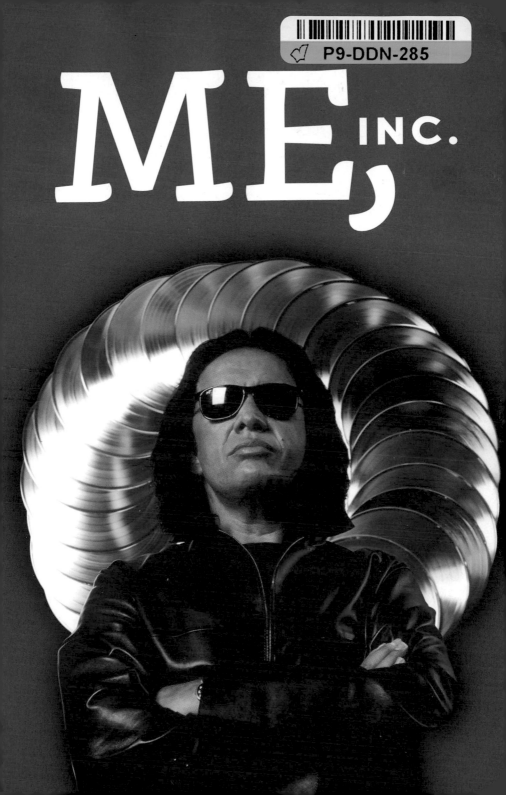

ME, INC.

Also by Gene Simmons

Nothin' to Lose: The Making of KISS (1972–1975),
with Ken Sharp and Paul Stanley

KISS Kompendium, with Paul Stanley

*Ladies of the Night: A Historical and Personal Perspective
on the Oldest Profession in the World*

Sex Money KISS

KISS: Behind the Mask

KISS and Make-up

KISS: The Early Years, with Paul Stanley

ME, INC.

BUILD AN ARMY OF ONE, UNLEASH YOUR INNER ROCK GOD, WIN IN LIFE AND BUSINESS

GENE SIMMONS

DEY ST.
AN IMPRINT OF
WILLIAM MORROW PUBLISHERS

To my mother, who taught me the value of a penny.

To my family, Shannon, Soph & Nick,
who taught me what life is all about.

And to America for giving this little immigrant boy all the
opportunities it gives to its native-born sons and daughters.

HarperCollins books may be purchased for educational, business, or sales promotional use. For information please e-mail the Special Markets Department at SPsales@harpercollins.com.

FIRST EDITION

Designed by Renato Stanisic

Library of Congress Cataloging-in-Publication Data has been applied for.

ISBN 978-0-06-232261-6

14   15   16   17   18   DIX/RRD   10   9   8   7   6   5   4   3   2   1

CONTENTS

FOREWORD

BY JOHN VARVATOS

I grew up in a suburb of Detroit. Five children and my parents in a three-bedroom, one-thousand-square-foot bungalow with one little bathroom. In this humble setting, I learned about the importance of family. I also learned about the importance of independence, and the hard work needed to gain it.

Paper routes, cleaning pools, cutting lawns, pumping gas—whatever it took to earn some cash to carve out my own identity in these tight surroundings. As early as I remember, it was music that provided me with the emotional space I needed and clothes that gave me an edge. My earnings went to the local record shop and clothing stores.

When I was fifteen, I got a job in a men's store, selling clothes and taking advantage of the employee discount. While others sold a single shirt, I was pulling together outfits and entire wardrobes for my customers, and making enormous commissions. At eighteen, I went to college and studied pre-med. I took out student loans and continued to work my way through school selling menswear. The pre-med curriculum turned into a science teaching degree. I was earning significantly more selling clothes than I could as a teacher, and so I decided to stay in fashion.

At twenty-five, I partnered in opening a men's store, and for the next three years became obsessed with learning everything

I could about running a business, being a buyer and merchant, and creating a brand. While doing this, I was noticed by the president of Ralph Lauren, who offered me a job heading up their sales division in the Midwest. A year and a half later, I was asked to move to New York and run the sales for the entire men's division. It was in this creative environment that, at the age of twenty-nine, a lightbulb went off and I discovered my true calling. I wanted to design the clothes that I had been selling for all those years.

I took chances, risks, and pay cuts to follow this calling. Five years later, I was head of design for all Calvin Klein men's brands. A few years after that, I returned to Ralph Lauren to head up men's design—one of the biggest jobs in global menswear.

In 1999 and in my forties, I left this amazing brand to start my own company, John Varvatos. With a fantastic team, we have created one of the top designer brands in the world. The road was, and continues to be, filled with bumps and bruises, but the rewards are worth the fight. I have been able to pursue and execute many of my passions: working with the biggest rock music artists on the planet, having my own radio show on Sirius XM satellite radio, designing a car for Chrysler, and publishing my first book on rock-and-roll and fashion. No one ever said it was going to be easy. Hard work, passion, vision, and continuing to raise the bar are all part of staying on top. Staying true to my vision and my brand is the golden rule.

While Gene Simmons's path has been quite different than mine, we share many similarities and I see in him a kindred spirit. We both have built brands that have unique identities and a clear DNA. We both have never forgotten where we came from. And just as important, our passion and commitment are stronger today than ever before. These values stand at the core of *Me, Inc.* and the hard-learned wisdom laid out here is a road map for success that anyone can benefit from.

John Varvatos has become a household name. His fashions are everywhere. My son, Nick Simmons, ran into him at an event and relayed the message that Varvatos would welcome the opportunity to work with KISS. Soon after, KISS flew to New York to do a photo session and play a special invite-only show. Little did I know that, prior to meeting John, he had excellent taste—not just in clothing, but in costume. The photo above is John Varvatos on January 1, 2000.

PREFACE

The first question you may ask is, "Who does this guy think he is? And why is a rock star writing a business book?"

Good questions. Keep reading.

Before we begin, let me point out that this book is designed to have two separate sections.

A "ME" section. As in ME, Incorporated.

And a "YOU" section. As in, YOU, Incorporated.

There's a little bit of "ME" in "YOU," of course, and there's a little bit of "YOU" in "ME." As it is with life. We're not so different.

At the end of each chapter in the "YOU" section you will also notice what I like to refer to as "The Art of More," which takes the experiences and advice I share in the book and boils them down to thirteen principles for success. Why thirteen principles? For one, I don't believe in luck as much as I do in hard work—but I'm also a fan of Sun Tzu's classic, *The Art of War*, which was divided into thirteen chapters. So you can consider these principles and this book an *Art of War* for winning the battles of everyday life.

You are welcome to skip my section (ME), and start reading your section (YOU). Or, you can read the book from the beginning—cover to cover. Both are fine. A word of caution, though: please don't use my experiences as a template or a short-cut for the hard work and self-education you will need in order to become a successful entrepreneur. My experiences and my journey have been mine alone. I had to educate myself. And I had to figure out the maze that lay in front of me, in order to rise to the top.

You will have to do likewise for yourself in order to rise to the top.

Take notes.

Ask questions.

Have group discussions.

Read the book with friends and family.

Talk about it.

Live it.

"Just Do It."

As I sit writing this, KISS has just been inducted into the Rock and Roll Hall of Fame, by a landslide vote from fans. This comes on top of getting our own star on the Hollywood Walk of Fame and keys to numerous cities; being allowed to ring the bell at both the New York and Toronto stock exchanges—well, all of it becomes almost more than I ever thought was possible, when my mother and I first set foot on this hallowed ground.

Though I was born in Israel, I can tell you that it's America that has become the Promised Land. Not just for me, but for people of all walks of life, all skin colors, and all nationalities. I will be forever indebted to this country for allowing me to breathe free, dream big, and achieve anything I ever imagined I could. And I want to thank America and its people for allowing this little immigrant boy's dreams to come true.

Now, go out there and make YOUR dreams come true.

ME,INC.

PART I
ME

1

A Young Entrepreneur

"The secret of getting ahead is getting started."
AGATHA CHRISTIE
English author and playwright

I f you've read my autobiography, much of this will sound familiar to you. However, even after we put our lives to paper, life moves on. I've gone through changes—with my family, my wife, and even the way I've chosen to view my distant past. All of the history you are about to read informed my identity as a businessman and an entrepreneur. So, even if you've heard it before, let's turn the clock back and remember.

Let's start with ME.

How did I get here?

I was born in Haifa, Israel, on August 25, 1949, in a hospital overlooking the Mediterranean Sea. My Hungarian mother and father had survived World War II and were able to escape to Israel, barely six months after it became an independent state.

My mother, Florence, was a survivor of the Nazi concentration camps. She was first imprisoned in the camps at age fourteen, and witnessed her mother and her grandmother walk into the gas chamber together. Her brother was also killed. My mother met my father, Feri Witz, in Jand, Hungary, right out of the concentration camps. In 1949, they were able to get to the new state of Israel.

When I was about seven years old, my father walked out on our family. What followed was the realization that, without him, the only ones that my mother and I could depend on were ourselves. Once the rug had been pulled out from under us, it was up to my mother—and then, eventually, up to me—to make a living. A hard enough life lesson to learn, but one that I learned at a very early age.

Life in Israel from 1949 through 1958 was hard. We lived in a one-bedroom apartment, with bullet holes in the walls from the various Israeli-Arab conflicts over the years. We didn't have a television at home. In fact, I had never even heard of TV and couldn't have imagined what it was.

We didn't have a bathroom. We had an outhouse, which was literally a hole in the ground. We didn't have toilet paper. We used rags, which were then washed and reused. We didn't have a bathtub or a shower stall. My mother would fill a metallic bathtub with water, pull it out into the sun to warm it up, and that was where I bathed. I had never heard of toothbrushes. Or toothpaste. Or tissues. When I finally learned that Americans used tissues, I was shocked to learn that you could blow your nose into a thin piece of paper and then throw it away. We used a handkerchief, and then we would wash it. Nothing was ever thrown out—we were dirt poor. We didn't have a car, and at the time I couldn't imagine anyone having one. You walked. Or you would take a bus. We didn't have a telephone. We couldn't afford one, so we didn't call anyone.

Food was rationed in Israel in the 1950s, because Israel was a new country (formed in 1948, the year before I was born). The infrastructure was in its infancy—running water was sporadic, and food was in short supply. There were certainly no brands as we are familiar with them here—bread was just bread. Butter was just butter. You'd get a certificate, and once a week you'd be allowed to purchase milk and a little bit of meat. No brand names, just milk and meat. You could also buy rice and bread, but I never saw brand names. All of the food at the grocery store was in big sacks. You would get a paper bag, or a newspaper, and then you would wrap up the food to take home. We didn't have a refrigerator. We had an ice box, which was a piece of furniture that functioned essentially like a cooler.

Despite the absence of luxuries in my early life, I was always happy. I still am. Growing up with little, it never took much to please me. My favorite thing in the world as a child was bread and jam. As long as I had my beloved bread with a heaping wad of jam on it I was happy. It's still the bane of my waistline. When I eat breakfast now, and the toast and jam comes, I smear it on, and Nick, Sophie, and Shannon always tease me about it. But the jam and bread goes back to my childhood and is a subconscious reminder that I actually don't need much to be happy, as long as I can sleep safely and soundly and have a full belly. Yes, I know this all sounds a little cornball, but perhaps it's a good thought to bear in mind as you start your journey to reach your entrepreneurial goals.

You actually don't *need* much. But that doesn't mean you shouldn't have it all.

My early years of school in Israel were uneventful. I attended kindergarten and grade school. I played in the dirt with rocks. We ran around and laughed. It was a happy time.

I have to confess, though, that I wasn't all that keen on going to school. One day, I decided to play hooky and hid out under the wooden one-story school building, and stayed there until school let out. Then I went home. Of course, I wasn't smart enough to pull the wool over my mother's eyes, and she soon found out I had lied. I learned another hard life lesson: lying doesn't work. In fact, I found out lying can be a pain in the ass. Literally.

I was a loner, mostly. And still am. We lived in the small village of Mount Carmel (yes, *that* Mount Carmel, the one in the Bible), which was very close to the city of Haifa. My mother couldn't afford to buy toys, and I was too young to care. I had a long stick and a rock, and those were my toys. I also had Mount Carmel— I could go hiking, and daydream. We couldn't afford to have pets, either, but when I was six years old I had a scarab beetle that I kept inside an old-fashioned matchbox, which I filled with sugar granules. The beetle was as much a companion to me as a cat or dog; I used to talk to it.

My journey as a young businessman, in this environment of minimal resources and opportunity, started out with a venture as small as you could imagine. One day, I'm not sure why or how, I came up with the idea of going up Mount Carmel and picking cactus fruit to sell to the people coming home on the buses that made their last stop at Tiraat HaCarmel, where we lived. I decided that I needed a partner and chose my friend Schlomo, a Moroccan boy my age who lived downstairs from us.

That was another good life lesson. Often, you won't be able to do it all yourself, so you will need to carefully pick a partner. Choosing the right partner is a very important decision, and can be the difference between success or failure. The person you choose should have the same work ethic as you do.

Schlomo and I spent the entire day up on Mount Carmel gathering the cactus fruit and hauling it down the mountain to the bus stop. We put the cactus fruit in a vat filled with ice and water, which we borrowed from the local grocery store, and sold it to the people who were coming home from work.

Both Schlomo and I felt a sense of purpose, a sense of pride, and a general feeling that we were doing something important. We didn't realize that it was a business venture, and we wouldn't have known what that phrase meant. But we *did* have a sense that if we worked hard, we *might* make money. And that was an exciting idea: *making money.*

It still is.

After a hard day's work, we were thrilled to find that we had made a grand total of two dollars (I'm simplifying the amount to spare you the math of converting from Israeli shekels, which was the currency at the time). Other than sweat equity, that is, the work that we'd put in, we had virtually no costs. Therefore, the entire two dollars was our net profit. We divided the amount, leaving me with one dollar. Remember, in 1956 a dollar was a decent amount of money. Today, the equivalent could be ten dollars, depending on how you adjust for the rate of inflation and monetary exchanges.

It was getting dark. Schlomo and I returned the vat that held the cactus fruit, and we hurriedly started the climb back up to where we lived. On the way, I stopped by an ice cream store and bought myself an enormous ice cream cone for two cents. To this day, I still vividly remember the taste. It was the most delicious ice cream cone I have ever had because it was mine and I bought it with my own money. Nothing tastes as sweet as something you've earned. And I still had a bulging pocketful of coins left.

When I got home, my mother was upset that I had been gone all day. Then I took out the coins in my pocket and put them on the table, and my mother stopped talking about how worried she'd been. The astonished look on her face will forever be etched in my mind. She cupped both hands over her mouth, eyes wide open, gave me a big hug, and said, in a hybrid of Hungarian and Hebrew, "That's my little man."

At that moment, although I was stinging from the cactus

pricks that covered my hands, arms, and face, I knew that work was good. Work resulted in money. Work and money resulted in food. Work and money resulted in happiness.

And that is the most profound capitalist lesson I have ever learned, though I was far too young to understand it at the time. All I knew was that I was proud. My mother was proud. And I had a huge ice cream cone I had worked to earn.

By the sweat of thy brow, the fruits of thy labor, or words to that effect. They're in a book my people wrote. It's the biggest-selling book of all time. Maybe you've heard of it: it's called the Bible.

With *Me, Inc.* I've written my own bible. One that I hope you'll find useful. Someday, you will write your own.

2

Coming to America

"There is no greater country on earth for entrepreneurship than America. In every category, from the high-tech world of Silicon Valley, where I live, to university R&D labs, to countless Main Street small business owners, Americans are taking risks, embracing new ideas and—most importantly—creating jobs."

ERIC RIES

Silicon Valley entrepreneur and author credited
with pioneering the lean start-up movement

In 1958, when I was eight and a half years old, I found myself on a plane with my mother, headed for New York. My uncle Joe had sent tickets for us to come to America. My mother told me not to worry, we were just going two stops and then we'd get off.

This was my first airplane ride, in a four-engine El Al Israel Airlines propeller plane. It was a bumpy ride and I kept throwing up. But I was surprised and delighted to find that you could just sit there and people brought food to you in your seat. I had never experienced that.

I still love that about planes.

After we landed at LaGuardia Airport, I was awed by the sheer size of everything. Everything I saw in America seemed bigger than I could have ever imagined. The buildings. The cars. The portions of food. The size of the people. Everything was big.

After our arrival, we moved into my beloved aunt Magda and uncle Larry's basement in their house in Flushing, Queens. Uncle Larry was my mother's brother. I was amazed that they had a refrigerator filled with food. Imagine that. It wasn't a restaurant, yet they had a refrigerator with food in it? I had never seen such a thing before. I couldn't fathom that they owned their own house, and had a car, and a bike, and a refrigerator full of food.

I was also introduced to Cocoa Marsh, a chocolate syrup, which I immediately fell in love with. I was even more impressed by a jar of jam. When my aunt Magda saw how awed I was by that jar of jam, she gave me a spoon and said to me in Hungarian (since she didn't speak Hebrew and I couldn't speak a word of English at the time), "Go on, taste it."

I thought she meant I could have all of it. So I ate the whole jar with a spoon.

My cousins Eva and Linda and my aunt Magda and uncle Larry and my mother were all laughing. I didn't know why. All I knew was that in my young life, I had never tasted something so wonderful.

And then there was Wonder Bread. Oh my Lord, how I loved that bread. To me, it was like cake. I would often eat the bread with nothing on it. And after I discovered *ketchup*, there was no stopping me. I ate ketchup sandwiches, which consisted of a big ketchup smear between two slices of Wonder Bread. I put ketchup on everything: on tuna fish, on scrambled eggs—everything. I still do.

Aunt Magda and Uncle Larry allowed my mother and me to live in their basement for two years, and I will forever be grateful. In our time there, I experienced many things for the first time:

riding a bike, brushing my teeth, bathing indoors in a bathtub. And for the first time, I sat on a toilet. This was also when I was introduced to toilet paper; I no longer had to use rags to wipe. The first time I used toilet paper, I threw it in the wastebasket. I didn't know you were supposed to flush it down the toilet bowl.

Every day was an amazing experience. The streets were filled with cars and people. The houses were neatly lined up next to each other. Everyone seemed happy and well fed. It was normal to see kids my age walking around with ice cream cones in their hands as if it were a banality. That treasure, an ice cream cone, which before I had worked so hard to attain, was old hat to these kids. It was humdrum. This is the luxury of America. It's all relative.

The first time I walked to the end of the street where Aunt Magda and Uncle Larry lived, I was afraid to cross. The streets were filled with cars going every which way. I had never seen a traffic light, so I didn't understand how one got to the other side. But when I saw people starting to walk across the street, I hurriedly followed them. And there, on the other side, I visited my first supermarket.

To say that I was in awe wouldn't do it justice. It was simply beyond anything I could have ever imagined. To me, it seemed like a city of food, with the crisscrossing aisles looking like streets filled with a level of abundance that was completely new to me. I had never imagined that you could choose from fifty different brands of coffee. In fact, I had never imagined that you could choose much of anything.

When my mother and I visited her other brother, Uncle George, and his wife, Florence, I saw my first television set. It was a huge piece of furniture, perhaps four feet wide, with cabinet doors on each side and a big curved screen in the middle. It must have been evening news time, because I remember seeing a black-and-white close-up of the face of a man inside the box. I envisioned a man inside the box talking to us. All I could do was stare at the screen, amazed at the wonder of television.

While visiting Uncle George and Aunt Florence, I wandered outside and walked down the street. At the corner, I was attracted to a striking bloodred metal structure. It wasn't all that tall, and there seemed to be a lever. I reached up and pulled it.

All hell broke loose. A bell began ringing like crazy. I stood frozen. Within a few seconds, I heard loud sirens coming toward me. I had never seen a street fire alarm before and I had never heard sirens, much less seen a fire truck. As I ran back toward Uncle George's house, I came upon the longest, largest vehicle I had ever seen. It was painted bloodred, just like that metal structure that was now making so much noise. It was bigger than a bus. And it had *two* drivers, one in the front and one at the back. The sirens scared the daylights out of me. I ran back into Uncle George's house and quietly sat in the corner, scared out of my mind. It sounds like an exaggeration, but I was truly an alien here. A stranger in a strange land.

My mother was always a proud, independent woman. Although her brothers George and Larry both offered housing and help, she decided that she and I would have to move and get our own place. She refused to accept loans and always insisted on earning her own way. She taught me to be that way. Never a borrower be.

To keep me off the streets, and before I had a mastery of the English language or knew anything about American culture, my mother moved us to Brooklyn. But she couldn't afford to get us an apartment, so she enrolled me in religious studies at Yeshiva Torah Vadas at Third Street and Bedford Avenue in the Williamsburg section.

It was a Jewish theological seminary, very conservative, and very entrenched in biblical studies. I was set up by the yeshiva to live with the Scheinlen family, who owned a bakery, while my mother lived with her brother Larry. They treated me as if I were a member of the family. I will forever be grateful to them for giving me a safe environment, and for giving my mother a chance to make some headway at work—she refused to take a handout, even then.

Yeshiva was hard. Six days a week, I would get up every morning at six, and would be at the yeshiva by seven thirty. We would start our day by praying at the temple, those of us who actually did pray. At eight thirty, we would begin studying American history, math, and English, and the rest of the day was spent studying the Bible. After 6 p.m., we would go back to yeshiva, eat our dinner, and then continue our Bible studies until 9:30 p.m.

I was eight and a half years old when I saw Santa Claus for the first time, on a billboard advertising Kent cigarettes. At the time, I had never heard of Santa Claus or Christians or Jesus Christ. Santa had a beard, was smoking a cigarette, and had a furry hat on his head, so I assumed he was a Russian rabbi. And then I started hearing the story of Jesus and how he was also a Jew, and a rabbi as well, and that none of the people who worshipped him were Jews. And that he was God *and* the Son of God, and that there was a Holy Ghost.

I was so mixed up. But I became interested in theology and different religious beliefs, so I started voraciously reading the New Testament and the Koran and other religious books. I learned about Islam and that it honored both Christians and Jews. I learned so much that now, when I meet religious zealots of all kinds, they find it very difficult to make their points, because I can quote psalm and verse right back at them. (Just a digression. Pride has always been my favorite sin.)

America was a whole new world that I could never have imagined, of different peoples with different beliefs, and all of them lived together. I was thrilled to find that America welcomed all sorts of people and gave immigrants the same rights as native-born Americans. This was astonishing to me, and it's one of the reasons why I love America to this day with all my heart.

I could read anything I wanted to. I could speak my mind. And my mother and I were safe, with no Nazis trying to kill us, no countries surrounding our border that wanted us to disappear— this freedom of expression was not, unlike where I came from, under constant threat of violent reprisal from a war you could literally hitch a ride to in a passing car.

Absorbing my new surroundings, I started to feel *strong*. I started to feel a *sense of being*. Some of that came from watching television. I saw that Superman could come from another planet, and still rise to greatness. I felt like—well, Superman. My *self-esteem* grew. I felt like I was *somebody*. Because America gave me the right to *be* somebody. What America had, was a "nothing is impossible" mind-set. You could see it on people's faces as they went off to work, and you could feel it when you watched TV and saw people flying through the air, and deflecting bullets. You could smell it. It was all around you. And the heroes who were championed were diverse in their origins. They need not have come from America—like Superman, who hailed from Krypton, and later on the Beatles, who hailed from England. From my young perspective, heroism seemed to be a meritocracy in a melting pot.

America taught me that no one is better than anyone else. And that, no matter the difference in your skin color, your accent, or your religious beliefs, no one has the right to make you feel less than what you are.

No one.

That feeling was one of the things that allowed me to forge ahead, and to never quit. This uniquely American spirit of individuality and pride allowed me to embrace the idea of entre-preneurship: that not only can you do anything—you can do ev-erything. It's also the feeling that allowed me, with my partner Paul Stanley, to form the band that we wanted to see, but never saw, onstage. But more about that band later.

3

Discovering TV and American Culture

After a year, my mother and I were finally able to move into an apartment a few blocks away from the yeshiva, at 99 South Ninth Street in Williamsburg, Brooklyn. Rent was thirty-five dollars a month.

We had few luxuries at home, but we did have a small television set. Once we got that TV, it felt like the world had suddenly opened up to me. I watched the evening news. I watched Superman. I watched cartoons. I watched movies. I learned more from television than any other medium I had ever encountered. More than books. More than teachers and school.

Television opened my mind to fantasy. To science fiction. To reality, through news coverage. Television was immediate. And *Adventures of Superman* in particular was a revelation—oh my God, that man is flying through the air, and he's not from

America—he's an immigrant, just like me! What television did and continues to do for me is to show me that there are no limitations to the imagination. There is no idea that is too outlandish to pursue—in business, and in life.

I'd spend my entire day at yeshiva, so I didn't have much time for TV watching on weekdays. But on the weekend—yes, even on the Sabbath, which for us was observed on Saturday—I would be glued to the TV set, often all day and as late into the night as I was allowed to watch. I would stay up and watch the screen go blank when the four or five local stations we had in those days went off the air.

Television also taught me how to speak with a "mid-Atlantic" accent. Mid-Atlantic is the sound of American English as spoken by newscasters around the country, whether they're from the Deep South (where a newscaster would never say "y'all") or the North (where a newscaster would never say "yo").

Having come to America not speaking a word of English, this fascinated me. So I started to mimic how TV newscasters spoke. I also noticed that they were always dressed better than the people on the street, and that they seemed to have an air of authority. So I learned to speak like them, without an accent, and even today, I've heard people comment that I sound like a TV broadcaster.

In 1959, a year after our arrival in America, I remember going to a friend's apartment in Brooklyn and seeing a tall pile of comic books stacked in a corner. I had never seen or heard of comic books before that day. At that point, I was still enrolled in yeshiva and trying to get a grasp of English, and I spoke what little English I knew with a deep Israeli accent. My friend and I sat down in front of this big stack, and he handed me my first comic book.

I still remember it clearly. It was *World's Finest Comics*, and it included Superman (the man I had seen flying through the air on television) and Batman. I was awed by the fact that these weren't just regular people. They were extraordinary people, leading extraordinary lives. And there was always good and evil.

I was hooked. I devoured comic books. I still do. So does the rest of the world, apparently. Comics, once a relatively small underground movement, are now recognized as an influential cultural and commercial force. Comic Con, held annually in San Diego, has grown from a one-day gathering attended by 145 people into a four-day event attracting hundreds of thousands of people, on a par with the Cannes Film Festival, and has inspired numerous spin-offs around the world.

In fact, the cultural power of the world of comic books, fantasy, and sci-fi can be seen in its current influence on pop culture, inspiring multimillion-dollar franchises such as *Star Wars*, *Superman*, *The Avengers*, *Avatar*, and *The Lord of the Rings*. All of those blockbuster Hollywood franchises arose from the same world of fantasy, sci-fi, and comic books that once seemed "kid stuff."

That first *World's Finest* comic book launched my love affair with comics. And as with any area that I become passionate about, I became voracious for the most minute trivia. I can quote you psalm and verse from the old testament of comic books. Off the top of my head, I know the history of the Hulk: the original gray Hulk, written by Stan Lee, drawn by Jack Kirby, and inked by Dick Ayers, which evolved into the green version, and then the red version, and I can tell you in which issues of *The Incredible Hulk* Steve Ditko took over art chores. Yes, the Spider-Man artist actually drew the Hulk for a while! And I can tell you all about Iron Man, who was likewise drawn by Jack Kirby and Dick Ayers, and I can tell you on which issues Don Heck later took over as artist. These were my modern myths, my Samsons, my Davids and Goliaths. These became my templates for good and evil, my archetypes of virtue.

In point of fact, I originally started doing my trademark "rock on" hand gesture—usually referred to as the "devil horns," which can now be seen in just about any sports stadium and rock concert around the world—in 1973 as an homage to Steve Ditko's Dr. Strange, who used the hand gesture to invoke his Magicks ("may the dreaded Dormamu invoke his wrath upon thee"). When Ditko's other creation, Spider-Man, shot his webbing from his wrist, the same hand gesture was used, but upside down.

What's more, I couldn't have imagined in my wildest dreams that America would allow me to actually *become* a comic-book superhero. *KISS* comics was published by Marvel Comics in the late seventies and became their biggest-selling comic book—at $1.50 a copy, when other comic books sold for twenty-five cents. The KISS comic book was magazine size, not comic-book size, so that it could be racked next to *Time* and the like. I'm proud to say that I got to fight Dr. Doom and meet the Fantastic Four with my bandmates in the first issue.

I also could never have imagined that someday I would have my own *Simmons Comics* line and the freedom to create *my own* comic-book characters and titles.

But I'm getting ahead of myself.

I was nine years old in 1959, and attending yeshiva six days a week. When I wasn't in yeshiva studying, I was at the library, which was about three blocks from it. I was delighted to find out that everything in the library was *free*. I didn't understand the historical significance of that then, but I do now.

For the first time in my life, I was in a place where the poorest of the poor and the richest of the rich have the same access to all information for free, on a level playing field. Without censorship. Without book burnings by the Nazis. Without being burned at the stake by those with different religious beliefs. Complete freedom and access to all information, art, and culture from around the world.

Then and there, I promised myself that I would educate myself, and that I would never *stop* educating myself. It was *my* responsibility to keep learning. I would spend hours at the library on the weekends and read everything I could get my hands on. Books on dinosaurs. Books on history. I almost read the entire *Encyclopaedia Britannica*. And all for free.

The reason I'm telling all of you this is that I want you to take this point to heart and make you understand that it's *your* responsibility to educate yourself. It's not important if you lack qualifications—go out and learn, and you will slowly amass qualification. No one is born qualified to do anything—it is all earned through hard work and education.

I had my beloved books. I had comic books. I had television. These were all part of my self-education. What more could I possibly need? I suppose I was sheltered, but my mother only had my best interests at heart in sending me to yeshiva. She wanted me off the streets and safe from early morning until late at night, when she returned home from a hard day of work. She would be up by the crack of dawn and home by seven at night, making the trek from Jackson Heights to Brooklyn every day to sew buttons for less than minimum wage. In that interim, she wanted to make sure I was safe—there were street gangs in our area, and being Jewish was not a popular thing. It has never been a popular thing. Arguably, it still isn't.

At the time, Williamsburg was a place where different cultures worked and lived together: Jews, African-Americans, Puerto

Ricans, and others. In today's parlance, you might call it a ghetto. Incidentally, most Americans are not aware that *ghetto* was originally a Venetian term used to describe the segregated neighborhoods where Jews lived. So this term has special significance to me.

Here's the background: During the Italian Renaissance, when Jews were making headway in the Italian city-states as craftsmen, traders, and merchants, the only part of the city in which they were actually allowed to live was in the *getta*, an area far from the center of town and where bricks were baked for buildings. There were huge brick ovens and men worked around the clock. Needless to say, the living conditions were horrible; there was smoke in the air day and night. This is where the term *ghetto* was born. And in World War II, when Polish Jews rebelled against the Nazi occupation, they were segregated into a section called the Warsaw Ghetto.

My mother worked six days a week in a sweatshop. No minimum wage. It was the only job available to her in New York with her skill level. She would lift a winter coat off a hanger, carry it to her Singer sewing machine, sew six to eight bottoms on that coat, hang the coat back on the hanger, and move it to another section. Then she would repeat that process, over and over again.

She made half a penny per button. So, if my sweet mother took down a coat, sewed six buttons on it, and then hung it up again, she would make a grand total of three cents per coat. Somehow, she was able to clear $150 a week doing this backbreaking work six days a week, and she was able to pay rent, buy food, and keep us clothed.

My mother was the best role model for a work ethic I could ever have. Through her, I was able to understand the value of money.

At the age of fourteen, I promised myself I was going to make something of myself, if only to make sure my mother would never have to work again. Within eight years, I would be able to substantially improve my mother's life. A few years after that, she would never have to work another day.

4

Discovering Junior Achievement and Learning About the Capitalist Business Model

"First, have a definite, clear practical ideal: a goal, an objective. Second, have the necessary means to achieve your ends; wisdom, money, materials, and methods. Third, adjust all your means to that end."
ARISTOTLE
Greek philosopher and writer (384–322 BC)

Unlike books, television, and comics, school, unfortunately, didn't teach me much.

That's because, generally speaking, most public school curriculums don't focus on real life skills. You never see courses such as How to Get a Job, or How to Balance a Budget, or What Should I Do for a Living?

Opportunity for financial success is all around us. It is there for us to take advantage of. It is there for us to reap the rewards. It is there, but too often we don't understand what it is or how it works. There's no mechanism in place in our society that, as a matter of course, teaches us how to recognize opportunity and capitalize on it. If you have the instinct for it, or happen into a scenario where someone is willing to teach you, then you're at a tremendous advantage.

My earliest jobs included delivering the *Long Island Star-Journal* and working the butcher block in Jackson Heights, Queens. Then, at the age of twelve, I was fortunate enough to enroll in Junior Achievement, and I finally got a real understanding of what the capitalist business model is and how things work. What the "price of goods" is. What "stock in a company" consists of. How one has to do a budget and try to slice off a small profit at the end. How taxes can cut your gross net profit dollars, if any, by a third or a half.

For those not already familiar with it, Junior Achievement is a nonprofit organization, founded in 1919 by Horace A. Moses, Theodore Vail, and Winthrop M. Crane, whose mission was to educate young people about free enterprise, entrepreneurship, and personal finance, and to allow teens to gain a hands-on understanding of how the capitalist model works.

One of Junior Achievement's many worthy endeavors is its after-school Company Program, in which a group of teens gather under the guidance of volunteer advisers from the local business community. Together the teens and the business leader craft their own business model. In essence, they form a company, and learn through practical experience how a business comes together, operates, and, hopefully, becomes profitable.

The company that my group formed was a cookie company. Simple enough, but how do we make money? How much does a cookie cost to make? How many hours does it take to make a cookie? How much do we pay partners and workers in the company? How and where can we sell the cookies? And to whom do we sell our cookies?

In forming our own company, we would decide on the bylaws of the company, that is, the rules under which our organization would operate. We would decide who would be our president, secretary, and treasurer, and who would be our CEO (chief executive officer) and COO (chief operating officer). If you don't know what these terms mean, go look them up and educate yourself. We would decide how many shares of our cookie company we would "sell" to potential investors (in other words, friends, family, anybody) in return for a share of our profits. We would decide how much a share in our company would cost.

We needed to sell shares to fund the company and had to figure out exactly how many shares we had to sell—and at what price—to raise enough capital to do so. We then had to make sure that we could sell enough cookies to turn a profit after covering the cost of buying sugar, the cost of buying flour, and the cost of the equipment that we would need to bake our cookies, etc. Another issue we had to deal with was taxes, which is something that we would all have to contend with when we grew up.

I took notes. I wrote things down. I noticed how I could apply many of the principles I learned from Junior Achievement in my own life and in my own future business ventures. I saw how I could apply it to my own "inferred fiduciary duty to myself"— that is, that it's my responsibility to minimize my financial exposure, and make sure that I outlay as little as possible and only for those things that I felt I truly couldn't do without. I realized that it's my responsibility to try to maximize my financial gain.

So I got it. I understood. I saw the light.

Other chapters in this book will explain my decisions, all based on limiting my financial exposure (spend little money) and maximizing my financial gain (make more money). But for now, suffice to say, the less I spent, the more I earned.

"A penny saved is a penny earned," said Benjamin Franklin.

Not quite, actually. A penny saved is two pennies earned.

Huh?

Well, any penny that you save and get to keep is a penny you have already paid tax on. Which means that, at the highest tax rate, you would have had to earn two pennies in order to have one penny remaining.

Your IRS "partner" walks, sleeps, and eats right beside you. With any penny or dollar you earn and save, the IRS will make sure it get its share.

What this really means is: spend as little as you can, and spend only for those things you can't live without, in order to have money left over.

5

My Early Jobs and Their Influence on Me as an Entrepreneur

"There is no substitute for hard work."
THOMAS EDISON
inventor of the phonograph, the motion picture camera,
and the practical lightbulb, and pioneer of electric power

As soon as I graduated from Newtown High School in Elmhurst, Queens, in 1968, I moved to South Fallsburg in upstate New York, to attend Sullivan County Community College, which is part of the State University of New York. During the summer months, and when I wasn't in class, I also worked part-time in Manhattan.

By this point, I understood the model: Spend little, earn more. Have the skills to earn myself more money. Know where to go to sell those skills. Educate myself. Learn people skills. Learn language skills.

In junior high school, I had noticed that all the girls took typing and stenography classes (steno being shorthand, that is, the thing that secretaries and court stenographers do). So I enrolled in both, because I wanted to improve my skills and because the classrooms were full of girls. By the time I graduated from high school, I could type faster than anyone I knew.

During the summer of 1968, I went to downtown Manhattan and got a job at Kelly Girl, Inc., later Kelly Services, Inc. It was a temporary job service that provided offices and corporations with staff they could hire and then let go of quickly. I could type faster than all the other Kelly Girl people. I could take steno. I could take Dictaphone dictation. I'd take the recordings, listen line by line through headphones, and type up what needed typing. It paid between $50 and $75 per week, part-time.

I also worked the night shift, from 8 p.m. until 6 a.m., on Wall Street at the Williamson & Williamson law firm. I filed, did office work, and typed up all sorts of reports. I would go to sleep by 8 a.m., if I could, and then get up at 2 p.m.

At college, I didn't have a car. I used to hitchhike upstate or back to New York City, or catch a ride to New York with fellow students who had cars. I couldn't see spending the money for a car. Or living off campus. All of it cost money. And I never wanted to waste or spend any money if I didn't have to.

While I attended Sullivan CCC, I worked for Zakarin Brothers in their warehouse, two blocks from the college. First I worked as a "humper," carrying boxes back and forth, and later as a manager of the floor activities. I earned $100 to $150 per week there.

Because I could type fast, I was able to start a typing service while at college, charging my fellow students fifty cents per page to type their papers. I had to turn away business. Nobody wanted to sit in front of their typewriter, especially since most of them never learned to type.

I typed fast and double-spaced, so it took me two or three minutes to type a page. In the course of an hour, I could make about $10. That was seven or eight times the minimum wage at the time. A fifty-page term paper might take me an hour and a half, and would earn me $25. Over a weekend of concerted effort, I could clear more than $100 and still have time to go on dates, and to concerts and restaurants.

On weekends when I wasn't doing my typing business—and while other boys my age would typically be relaxing, screwing around, and otherwise slacking off—I worked as a lifeguard at the Pines hotel in South Fallsburg. That job paid about $70 to $100, because I also called the bingo numbers to a roomful of women, and got tips for that.

I didn't have the expense of owning a car. I had no rent to pay. I had no girlfriend, though I had plenty of dates. I bought almost nothing. I still don't buy much for myself that I don't need.

I didn't socialize much. If I wanted companionship, I would simply ask a girl if she wanted to come over to help me type up papers. Presto, a date! I had female companionship, and I could stay in my room and continue to earn money. Kill two birds with one stone, as the saying goes.

I was almost nineteen when I joined a college rock band called—*gulp*—Bullfrog Bheer. The band played beer bashes, which were exactly what you'd imagine them to be. People listened to music, rocked out, and drank beer. The band played a mix of the songs of the day, along with some of the original songs that I'd started to write. Despite the fact that I had already started playing bass, I wound up on rhythm guitar in the band, because they already had a bass player.

We would get paid between $150 and $300 for playing beer bashes, and would play two nights on most weekends. So after splitting the money with the three other guys in the band, that was another $75 to $150 for me.

Between my typing money, the weekend band money, and the Zakarin Brothers money, in a good week I could make $500, which was decent money at the time. Not every week, mind you, but enough weeks that it allowed me to pay off some of the college loan that I'd taken out to avoid burdening my mother with that responsibility (and, since I paid it early, I paid less than I could have). God knows that she'd already done more than any mother should be expected to do for a son.

During the summer months of 1969, when I had time off from college, I worked at the Direct Mail Advertising Association. DMAA's angle was asking consumers what junk mail they did not want to receive—junk mail meaning the samples, ads, circulars, and other stuff that you get in the mail that you never asked for—and getting them to respond. And it worked. You let DMAA know which junk mail you did not want, and magically, you stopped getting it.

So DMAA was on *your* side, right? Well, yes and no. What DMAA actually did was to compile a list of people who didn't want ads or samples of certain types of products sent to them in the mail. DMAA would then sell that list to companies, who would use it to fine-tune their mailing lists of who received junk mail relating to those products. In essence, the DMAA would help companies to more accurately market their products to people who would be more inclined to be interested in them. Win/win. People stopped receiving unsolicited stuff they weren't interested in, and the companies learned more about people who *might* be interested in buying their stuff.

I also worked as a proofreader at R. R. Bowker, which published *Publishers Weekly* and *Library Journal*, and as an assistant at *Glamour* magazine. They liked me at *Glamour*. I knew pop culture. I was a wiz at typing. I could take dictation. I could fix mimeograph machines and Rexograph machines, thanks to all the experience I'd gotten after my dear mother bought me both of those duplicating machines so I could publish my fanzines. As a history buff, I could cross-collateralize pop culture trends with historical references.

After graduating from Sullivan CCC with my associate of arts degree in 1970, I moved back to New York to pursue my bachelor's degree in education at Richmond College in Staten Island, which was part of the City University of New York. I moved back into my mother's house in Flushing, Queens. For a twenty-one-year-old, it wasn't the coolest thing to do, but I didn't care.

Apparently, the Condé Nast staff took note of my skills, because after I graduated from college in the summer of 1972, I found work as assistant to Kate Lloyd, the editor of *Vogue*. A nice perk of the job was that I was the only male on the floor. The *Vogue* offices were filled with models coming in and out of their fittings and photo sessions, and most of them were my age. I was fortunate to make new friends.

I had begun amassing a decent amount of money. So much so that I was able to "loan" some money to my mother and her new husband, Eli, for a down payment on a home. A few years after that, I was able to buy my mother her own home and car.

I was not ready to start paying rent or to buy a car or for any of the other costs incurred when you go out on your own. I needed to finish my college education. So I decided to stay at home with my mother, who I'm glad to say was happy to have me. I also contributed to the household expenses.

Living at my mother's home while attending Richmond College wasn't easy. To get from my mother's home in Flushing, Queens, to Staten Island, I'd have to get up every morning at six, take the bus to the last stop at Main Street in Flushing, and then take the subway to the very last stop at the tip of Manhattan Island. From there I would have to catch the ferry, which would travel past the Statue of Liberty and finally arrive at Staten Island. The trip from home to campus took two hours each way. That's four hours of travel on every day I attended college.

That didn't leave me much time to get a part-time job, or for many other activities. I had already started playing in a band called Wicked Lester, with Paul Stanley and my junior high school friend Stephen Coronel (with whom I would write the songs "She" and "Goin' Blind"), but we were just getting started and had yet to make any money.

So I came up with a way to make money by buying and selling comic books. Since I knew the value of certain titles and dates, I put my old mimeograph machine to work and printed up a circular announcing that I would pay a dollar per pound for old comic books. The circular had my phone number on it, and I started getting calls immediately. Since I couldn't drive, Paul Stanley did me the favor of driving me around in his Mustang. We would pull up to a house, I would pay the owner in cash, and then walk away with stacks of old comic books.

It was a good business. If I paid ten dollars for ten pounds of comics, the chances were that one of those comic books, with the right title and the right date and the right quality, could fetch thousands of dollars. One of the finds that came from someone's attic was an old issue of *Action Comics*, the title that debuted Superman. It may have been number fifty-eight or so, but the condition was good. And that meant I could resell it to a collector or comic book store. I knew of a collector who owned his own store in Elmhurst, Queens, next to the high school I attended (Newtown High School), and after much haggling (and after he saw that I knew what it was worth), I sold it to him for around $800. This is the inferred fiduciary duty to myself that I mentioned, and will mention again—I knew what the book was worth because I did the research. Otherwise, he might have short-changed me—and it wouldn't be his responsibility to correct me. The onus was on me to make sure I knew the value of my merchandise.

In the fall of 1972, I began working at the Puerto Rican Interagency Council, a government-funded research and demonstration project. Its goal was to find out how government funding was being used to help Puerto Ricans in the northeastern United States. I ran the office, which was located on Lexington Avenue and East Ninety-Fifth Street in upper Manhattan, and I was the assistant to the two women who headed the project, Magdalena Miranda and Leticia Diaz. I had the keys, and I was responsible for opening the office, answering phones, typing missives, fixing the mimeo and Rexograph machines, whatever had to be done.

The report that we worked on was titled *Improved Services to Puerto Ricans in the Northeast USA and Puerto Rico*. I should know what the report was called, because I typed every single word of it. I still proudly have a copy. On the first page is the list of the people who participated in the project. All the way at the bottom of the list, there's my name, Gene Klein, as I was known at the time.

After my workday ended at the Puerto Rican Interagency Council, I would take the subway downtown to Fifth Avenue and Fourteenth Street to a deli, where I manned the checkout counter. I would work there until 10 or 11 p.m., for two dollars per hour. I could also eat as much as I wanted, and could even take out food with me.

Then, around 11 p.m., I would take the subway uptown a few blocks to 10 East Twenty-Third Street, where Paul Stanley and I were starting to rehearse with Wicked Lester. We'd play until one or two in the morning. It wasn't a particularly glamorous section of New York. And it's not much to look at now. But all we knew in 1972 was that there was a second-floor loft, with no windows and one door, and it was cheap. Paul and I arranged to rent the rehearsal loft for the grand sum of two hundred dollars a month. The elevator hardly ever worked and we were forced to climb the stairs and haul our amplifiers. But it's where the seeds of our success were sown. And we worked at it relentlessly.

Each night, after we'd finish rehearsing, I'd head out to my mother's new home in Bayside, Queens. Bayside was far from Manhattan and I would have to take the subway to the last stop in Queens, then hop on a bus and take that to the last stop in Flushing, which took an hour and twenty minutes. Eventually, I moved my bed and a TV set into our rehearsal space in Manhattan, aka "the Loft." That way, we could rehearse as late as we wanted to and I could still be up at 7:30 a.m. and at work at the Puerto Rican Interagency Council by 8:45 a.m.

They say "never put all your eggs in one basket." On Wall Street, they say "spread the risk." It's kind of the same thing. And, though I wasn't trained in this area, I seemed instinctively to know certain precepts of good business practice. I wanted to try for a career in the music industry, otherwise known as forming a rock band. But there was no guarantee it would work. In fact, statistics should have been enough to tell me the cards were stacked against me. So I worked at two jobs at the same time I was trying to put together the band. I worked at the Puerto Rican InterAgency Council, as assistant to the Director. And then after 5:00 p.m., I would take the New York subway system down to Fourteenth Street and work at a delicatessen, as the checkout person (the person you paid, before you left). I also was allowed to eat there and take food with me, as well as being paid. By the time KISS started, I had amassed $23,000, because though I wanted to pursue a passion, I refused to gamble with my livelihood. The gamble would have paid off, as it turns out—I would soon have to quit my various jobs, because our new band would start taking up more of my time. Within a year and a half, we would be playing Anaheim Stadium in California. But that doesn't mean it would have been wise to put all my hopes in one area, sink or swim. The lesson I learned while working two additional jobs alongside the band was one I would implement later, even after the band—and it was a lesson that would save me, time and time again. Spread the risk. Play to win.

6

Who Am I?

"Whether you think you can or whether you think you can't, you're right!"
HENRY FORD
industrialist, founder of the Ford Motor Company,
and developer of the modern assembly line

I invented myself.

At birth, I was given the name Chaim Witz. Witz (pronounced *Vitz*) was my father's last name.

To most Americans, my given first name, Chaim, sounds like a cat coughing up a hairball. That's because the Hebrew guttural "ch" sound (probably the most common sound in the Hebrew language) is unknown in English and in most Romance/Latin-derived languages—except perhaps German, which has its own, slightly less guttural "ch" sound.

At any rate, it didn't take me long after our arrival in America to realize that my Hebrew name simply didn't work here. No one knew how to spell or pronounce it, for the same reason that people in Western society also have a hard time spelling or pronouncing the name of the Jewish holiday Chanukah, the Festival of Lights.

So, I decided to *change my name.*

That's right.

Just like that.

If I ask you what your name is, chances are you'll tell me. But I'm here to tell you it's not *your* name. You had nothing to do with choosing it. It was likely chosen for you before you were even born.

I decided I would have my own name. One that I would give myself.

Few things in life are choices. You can't pick where you're from. You can't pick the color of your skin. You can't pick if you're born male or female. So I decided that I would reinvent myself and I started with choosing my own name.

I picked Gene, probably because of Gene Barry, the 1950s and '60s actor who starred on TV in *Bat Masterson* and *Burke's Law* and in the sci-fi movie *War of the Worlds*. I thought Gene Barry was cool, so I became Gene.

When my mother divorced my father, she went back to her maiden name, Klein, in keeping with Jewish tradition. So when I left yeshiva and entered public school in the fifth grade, I became Gene Klein. I no longer needed to keep spelling or pronouncing my name whenever I introduced myself. My new name made me feel less like an outsider, less foreign.

However, while I liked the sound of Gene Klein a lot more than the sound of Chaim Witz, it still didn't resonate all the way for me.

I was Gene Klein from grade five through college graduation, up until the time I met Paul Stanley in 1972. Paul also had a different name at the time, and he changed it to Paul Stanley. Smart.

When it looked like I was going to be in a rock band, it became crystal clear to me that Jewish-sounding names simply didn't resonate for the masses in America, or in the rest of the world for that matter.

I'm not here to say whether it's right or wrong, or whether

it shouldn't matter what your name sounds like or if it's easy to spell. But it *does* matter, whether you like it or not.

I didn't take it personally. I recognized the facts. I realized that Robert Zimmerman had turned himself into Bob Dylan. That Marc Bolan from T. Rex had been born Mark Feld. And that Leslie West from Mountain had originally been known as Leslie Weinstein. They all reinvented themselves, changing their names, and their images along the way.

It was clear I needed to finish creating myself. Honestly, I can't remember where the name Simmons came from but it sounded American to me, and I wanted to *be American.*

So, in 1971, I became Gene Simmons. I remember it clearly. After a night of rehearsing with our new band, Paul and I were riding the subway back to our homes in Queens. (Neither of us could afford our own homes at the time; Paul lived with his parents and I lived with my mother.) It was past midnight and I remember telling Paul that I was going to change my name to Gene Simmons.

And just like that, I reinvented myself.

I also didn't look like I was in a rock band. Rock bands looked like they came from England, and were mostly white. I'm not here to give you the socioeconomic reasons; I'm just telling you that that's the way it was. And that's the way it still is, for the most part. In life and in business, it's always important to recognize what the predominant pattern is. That's just good market research. Remember, we're not just talking about recording artists; I'm talking about *rock stars.*

In the modern rock era (from 1962 onward), the vast majority of rock stars were young and white. There were virtually no African-American rock stars. There are barely any still, depending on how you define "rock star." One of the few exceptions was

Jimi Hendrix, although it bears noting both his bandmates were white and British.

There were never any Asian rock stars with the same worldwide appeal—not from India, Japan, China, or anywhere in Asia. There were never any Hasidic rock stars. And aside from perhaps Janis Joplin, there were never female rock stars of the magnitude of the Beatles and Elvis.

The few Jewish rock stars there were changed their names and/or downplayed the fact that they were born Jewish. They understood the masses didn't care, and that waving the Jewish flag was a turnoff. The masses just wanted *rock stars*.

We're talking *rock* here, mind you. Not pop or disco or new wave or any other form of music. R-O-C-K.

You needed to be a band. You needed to write songs and play your own instruments. You needed to have guitars, bass, and drums. And you needed to be young, white (there, I said it) men. I'm not here to make a value judgment on this fact—it might be a terrible result of whitewashing media, or some awful, unfair acts of subtle racism in pop culture. Whatever the cause—I wanted to succeed. If they wouldn't bow to me as I was, I would become something else. I would beat them at their own game.

R&B, meanwhile, was black. The Temptations, the O'Jays, and many others, all gloriously black.

The Beatles, the Stones, Led Zeppelin, and the rest of the rock stars at the time were all young white males and had a certain aesthetic. I didn't have that look. I wasn't quite "white." Not in the way the Brits were. So I did the best with what I had. I grew my hair. I learned to straighten it and blow-dry it, and used lots of hair spray. I still do. I started wearing loud clothes and taught myself how to write songs and how to play guitar and bass.

In 2012 Jimmy Page had come to check out KISS when we played London, England. And a year or so afterward, I had to be in New York on business. Jimmy, who happened to be in New York and was ever the gentleman, came over to say hello. The man who single-handedly came up with more classic riffs than all the other bands combined. The Riff Meister of them all.

I didn't know anything about marketing, and had never heard the term. But I instinctively knew what worked and what didn't work, without asking others. Either you do market research, or you have a gut instinct. I had, and continue to have, "gut instinct." My gut has served me well and has made me a good living.

Rock stars didn't just *look* like rock stars. Their names *sounded* like rock stars. Mick. Jimi. Yeah, "that rocks." There was something intangibly cool about those names.

All of these artists invented themselves. From head to toe, inside and out.

So I decided that if I was going to be in a band, I could increase my chances of success by choosing someone like Paul Stanley, who could be my partner. He was just as passionate about pop culture and success as I was. He was willing to create himself. We were both willing to become chameleons and do whatever it took to *become* the image that best worked for us in the marketplace that we wanted to be in. Top to bottom.

Look like a rock star, act like a rock star, and if you're lucky, you might get to *be* a rock star. Fake it till you make it.

When I taught sixth grade in Spanish Harlem, I was known as Mr. Klein. And that was an appropriate name for that job; it sounded like a teacher's name. But Klein was never going to work in a rock band. It simply didn't *sound* very rock and roll.

Gene Simmons wasn't perfect, but it was better than Chaim Witz, and since 1971, I have been Gene Simmons.

So far, so good.

7

KISS

On February 21, 1974, the first KISS album was released. That's forty years from this writing! What a crazy trip it's been.

But, by the summer of 1972, it looked like Wicked Lester wasn't going to work, even though we had a recording contract with Epic Records. So Paul Stanley and I regrouped and started again. We walked out of our Epic Records contract. We disbanded Wicked Lester! This time, we would put together the band we never saw onstage, the band that *we* wanted to be. This time, we would make sure we had the right lineup. This time, we would make sure we had the right songs.

We did it the right way.

We self-funded the band. We had no other partners. There were no investors. There was only us. Mostly, there was only Paul and myself.

This time we were going to do it for real.

Go big, or go home.

But we had no manager. We had no record label for our new band. We had no lawyers. We had no one to advise us or guide us.

So I began religiously reading the music-industry trade publications *Billboard*, *Cashbox*, and *Record World*. Every week,

I would see what the charts reported on what was selling and what was not. Every week, I learned which band was playing at which concert venue and how they did financially. Every week, I would learn about different music industry figures, who they were, what they did, and how they did it.

It was another type of education you were not going to get in school. And it's worth noting that what I was doing, although I probably wasn't familiar with the phrase at the time, was my own "due diligence," meaning that I educated myself.

As I've discussed, I always had a job or two, and was always saving money. So by mid-1972, when I was twenty-two years old, I had been able to save $23,000, which was a hefty sum in those days (still is for most twenty-two-year-olds). This is also part of due diligence—to educate oneself, and feed oneself, is one's own responsibility.

Paul owned a beat-up old Mustang, but more often than not, we both used the subway and buses for transportation. We ate hot dogs at the corner of Twenty-Third Street and Broadway. We never went shopping for clothes. We hardly spent any money at all.

But when it was time to get a loft to serve as our band's rehearsal space and base of operations, we didn't hesitate. The rent was two hundred dollars a month. In 1972, Ace Frehley and Peter Criss both joined our new band, which we were still calling Wicked Lester.

Peter was married and didn't work beyond pursing life as a professional musician. He was fortunate to have a wife, Lydia, who supported them both and was devoted to his quest to become a successful drummer in a band. That left rent monies for Paul and myself to cover. Sometimes Paul couldn't come up with his end, so it was up to me to make sure the rent was paid every month.

The band needed amplifiers. Paul and I bought them.

We needed a sound system. Paul and I bought a Peavey 27-input soundboard and sound speakers, and had friends build the sound system cabinets. It was cheaper. Paul and I paid for all of it. We didn't have roadies, so friends of Ace and Peter would usually help out.

Again, a good move. Invest in yourself. If you can afford it, don't borrow. Pay for it yourself.

By Christmas 1972, we rechristened ourselves KISS. Paul thought of the name. It was Ace who drew the band's first logo. Paul would later refine the logo, and that's the version we use on everything to this day.

I hit the phones and got us a few small clubs to play at and Paul had to go out and rent some milk trucks so we could haul the equipment to and from our shows.

Despite some early omens from Ace and Peter, we were young and thought of it all as a great adventure.

This brings us back to what I've been telling you about the importance of finding the right partners. You can't do it all yourself, and neither could any of us. Each of us on our own could only go so far. Together, we would go all the way.

By early 1973, it was time to put together a press package to proclaim KISS's birth and to invite the music industry to our coming-out concert at the Diplomat Hotel's Crystal Room. We were second on the bill. The Brats, a popular local band, were the headliners. Third on the bill was a band called Luger.

I wrote up a contract for all the bands to sign. I wasn't a lawyer and had no legal training. Why I thought it would be legally binding (it was) or why I thought the other bands would sign (they did) is beyond me. The contract said that each band would go on at a certain time and be off the stage by a certain time. Luger would go on at 8:30 p.m. and be off by 9:15. KISS would go on at 9:30 and be off by 10:30. The Brats, who were headlining, wouldn't hit the stage until 11 p.m.

All well and good.

I was still working at the Puerto Rican Interagency Council offices, and had the run of all the office equipment after hours. So when it was time to assemble our press package, I commandeered the typewriters, manila envelopes, and stamps and put together a big mailing to all the record labels, managers, music magazines, and music professionals whose addresses I could find in the year-end issues of *Billboard, Cashbox,* and *Record World.*

We made sure that none of the other bands' names were on the invites that I sent to music industry people. The press release only mentioned *Heavy Metal Masters "KISS"* and our set time, 9:30–10:30. The media and music managers who showed up were undoubtedly impressed when they saw the large room filled with fans. Most of them were probably there to see the Brats, but that fact would never be known to the industry people who attended the show.

A friend of Peter's who worked at a printing shop did us a favor and allowed us to reproduce posters advertising our show, which Paul and I posted on the sides of buildings around Manhattan to help build word of mouth. And Paul and Peter arranged to create black T-shirts with the KISS logo in glitter, and Peter's sisters wore them at the front of the stage, screaming for us.

Then, KISS hit the stage and tore it up. Afterward we were left with a half hour to meet and greet the music industry people and then get them out of there before the actual headliner hit the stage and our little ruse was exposed. The point: create your own hype. Whether you're in a band, or you're a mere salesman—make them believe in you. Make them believe they are the last to the party and it's started without them. You don't have to lie, but you do have to craft an image that makes people want what you have.

I met with Bill Aucoin right after our show at the Diplomat

Hotel, and he and I sat down to quickly chat. I arranged for a girl I had been "seeing" to sit on my lap as we spoke, to give the illusion of rock star grandeur I so admired in my heroes. And the die was cast. It worked like a charm. Bill immediately wanted to be involved. At the time, he was then producing and directing a TV show called *Flipside*, which interviewed John Lennon and other music personalities in the studio. He also produced a TV game show called *Supermarket Sweep*.

Aucoin agreed to become our manager. Contracts were drawn up, and KISS needed a lawyer. We hired Stan Snadowsky, a lawyer and music promoter who booked shows at the Bitter End, a club in Greenwich Village. He would always let us come into the club to see acts (the following year, Snadowsky would become co-owner of a new club, the Bottom Line, which would become a fixture of the New York music scene for three decades). Aucoin needed a lawyer as well, but didn't have funds to pay for his side, so I loaned him the money to pay his lawyer. I also paid all the KISS legal fees. All of my frugality was paying off—literally. With the substantial amount of money I'd saved, I was able to cover a lot of these early expenses that helped launch our career. No one else in the band had access to cash—and even our new manager was short on funds—so it was left up to me.

Within six months, in the fall of 1973, we were recording our first album for Casablanca Records with producers Kenny Kerner and Richie Wise at the legendary Manhattan studio Bell Sound, right down the street from Studio 54. We were young. We were inexperienced. And we simply couldn't believe what was happening to us.

Between the two jobs I had at the time, I was clearing close to $300 per week, a large sum at the time. When I quit my jobs so I could devote my full-time attention to KISS, I went from $300 a week to the $75 weekly salary that the band now paid me. That's what we all got at the beginning, although within a few months our salary was raised to $85—and that was before taxes.

But it didn't matter. We were doing what we loved. We were in a band. And we believed in what we were doing.

If I didn't have the cushion of my savings from all those other odd jobs, I might have continued working and not have been able to put my full focus into getting KISS to the next level. "Don't quit your day job" is often good advice, unless you can afford to do otherwise.

The story of KISS has been told and retold in books, movies, and documentaries. So I won't go into all of that here. Instead, I will return to my earlier observations about my apparent lack of formal qualifications for any of the business endeavors that I have pursued, beginning with music.

The field of popular music is populated mostly by unqualified people. They never went to school to learn what they do. In fact, they barely understand what they do, or how they do it. *They just do it.*

I can't read or write music, but I have written hundreds of songs.

I have never had music lessons. I have never had a music teacher show me how to play guitar or bass or keyboards or drums, although I dabble in all of them well enough to be able to write songs and record demos.

And I'm hardly alone in my lack of musical qualifications. In fact, I'm in some very good company, including many of music's most iconic figures.

Elvis Presley couldn't read or write music. The Beatles never learned to read or write music, and never took lessons to learn to play their instruments. They simply taught themselves.

You can go down the list. Jimi Hendrix, the Beatles, the Rolling

Stones, Foo Fighters, Green Day. Many of them are self-taught—
many of them never took formal lessons, yet they have no problem
writing and playing their songs. It's like learning to speak a new
language, but never learning to read or write it.

My point is that, in whatever field one chooses, it's up to *you*
to educate yourself to become an effective entrepreneur. And you
can't use a lack of formal training as an excuse not to pursue the
success that you desire.

I noticed early on that this thing that I had entered was never
just called music. It was always called the music *business*. And
show *business*. And the movie *business*.

Intrinsically, *everything* is a business.

Everything has, or should have, a balance sheet.

Everything has, or should have, a budget.

Everything has, or should try to have, a profit motive.

Work. Religion. Rock bands.

And YOU.

YOU are the business.

YOU should have a budget.

YOU should have a balance sheet.

YOU should have a profit motive.

I did then.

And I do now.

8

Learning About Branding and the Music Business

From the get-go, KISS understood that we were a business but there was still a lot to learn. Bill Aucoin and our lawyers helped us to learn about all sorts of new business areas that we'd never contemplated before.

Like trademarks. In order to protect our face-paint designs and our logos and our songs, we needed to trademark and copyright them. Trademark and copyright are slightly different legal terms, and they do slightly different things legally. But they're both designed to prevent others from stealing or copying your creations.

Copyrighting a song was standard practice at the time but trademarking our specific look was a whole other matter. No one had ever done something like this before. We were able to trademark our *faces*, and the way the makeup was designed on those faces. Before KISS, the creators of comic-book and cartoon characters could trademark what their creations looked like. But it was rare to make such a specific attempt to trademark what was, essentially, a living human being's stage identity. KISS manager

Bill Aucoin made us aware of the possibility of trademarking our actual faces. It took about a year and it was registered in 1977 with the Library of Congress. It's worth noting, Jimmy Fallon can't trademark his face—it's just a face. But KISS's faces are more than faces: they are symbols that have spanned four decades—and will likely survive our passing. It was the single biggest decision we ever made—because we incorporated a design into our faces, our faces became part of the design, and were therefore subject to trademark law. And these symbols have endured.

The lawyers explained "streams of income," that is, areas that pay you money. Royalties that the band would earn from our record sales. Money that we would receive for playing live concerts. Writing and publishing royalties generated by radio airplay of the songs we wrote and published, as well as their use in TV, films, and other media.

It became clear to Paul and myself that since we wrote almost all of the songs, we would be due more of the writer and publisher income than Ace and Peter. However, Bill Aucoin convinced us to split all monies four ways, including writer/publisher royalties. Bill was convinced that an even split would spur all four members to contribute more and work harder for the band, and to be selfless in doing whatever was needed to help make the band a success.

It was a nice idea, but sadly the reality was different. Even though we shared our writer/publisher royalties equally with Ace and Peter, this hardly seemed to inspire them to give their all to the band. Whatever dysfunction existed with Ace and Peter seemed to get worse. Much worse. And fast.

Respectfully, neither Ace nor Peter seemed to notice or care that Paul and I were making a gesture we didn't have to make. So an album or two later, we renegotiated and legally changed how our writer/publisher royalties would be divided. We should have been more forthright from the very beginning, but we wanted to make everyone in the band feel equal.

In the Who, Pete Townshend receives more money than Roger Daltrey. As well he should. He writes the songs.

A lesson learned: get paid for what you do.

In the midst of negotiations, formations, reassignments, and all of the above, KISS became the Gallup poll's most popular band for three years in a row. We beat out Led Zeppelin and even the Beatles.

Yet despite this success, we were routinely lambasted by critics for not adhering to some hypothetical code they made up called "credibility." An interesting idea, because no one could quite figure out who came up with it, what the rules were, who decided if you had cred, and so on. It had something to do with not focusing on making money—I hope you can see that from my point of view (the little immigrant boy who discovered how good it felt to sell cactus fruit and make my own living), this still sounds like nonsense. From the outset, KISS was a different type of band. We saw our fans wanted more than just records and concerts, so we gave it to them. We hear and we obey. T-shirts. Hats. Anything they wanted, we gave it to them. Supply and demand wasn't a shallow way to take advantage of people—it was about figuring out what people wanted, and providing it, without anyone's permission on what was "classy" or "credible." These people like us? These people actually want to buy things with our faces on them? I can actually make my living this way? Great.

KISS pioneered the idea that a rock band could become a *brand*. And this allowed us to explore even more revenue streams and handle a lot of it ourselves so we didn't lose money to an intermediary. We put order forms inside our albums, so fans could order T-shirts and belt buckles and all sorts of other items directly from us. We also made a deal with a gent named Ron Boutwell, who ran an order fulfillment warehouse in Los Angeles, from which our merchandise was shipped directly to the fans.

We published our own fan magazine, and we weren't shy about licensing and merchandising ourselves and our images, like no band had ever done before. Critics be damned.

And, of course, we were criticized for it by people who had never achieved anything, had never played in a band or written songs themselves. They simply had access to a typewriter and had a column. We ignored them. Then. And now. They mean nothing. Never have. Never will.

KISS would continue, decade after decade, going where no band had gone before. Nothing deterred us, not the critics and not even the loss of some of our founding members.

We chose to carry on, and continued to have great success with new members who regarded being in the band as an honor and a privilege. As of this date, Tommy Thayer and Eric Singer have been in the band longer than any lineup—we are KISS reborn. And with Paul, as the brother I never had, there is nothing we can't do. It's almost 2015! Watch us burn rubber.

Again, always make sure you have the right partners.

The lesson for you? Never let anyone or anything stop YOU, in your quest for success.

By the late seventies, KISS had become a worldwide phenomenon, and with our popularity came the flood of critics and naysayers who almost inevitably come along with success. I recall being backstage preparing for a concert in the South, when a well-intentioned but misguided preacher and his followers arrived at the concert hall's backstage entrance. The preacher was carrying a cross on his back—no, I'm not exaggerating, he really was carrying a cross on his back. I suppose I'd be a hypocrite if I said he was being too theatrical.

I was curious, so I opened the door. There he stood, dressed in what he presumably believed was the costume of the day for Jews in Hebron around AD 30. He pointed his finger at me and began to make accusations. I was going to hell, he said.

I asked him, kindly, whatever happened to "Do not judge, lest ye be judged?" I asked, who are *you*? What have you ever done? After a fairly lengthy theological debate, in which I stubbornly and relentlessly refused to just let him go, he retreated.

My real point here—with this story, and the critic-bashing—is that it's important to know, if you're going to be a success, that *no one* is better than you are.

No one has the right to shake his finger in your face.

No one is allowed to make you feel bad about yourself.

No one is better or holier than you are.

No one.

9

I Am an Entrepreneur

"Genius is 1 percent inspiration and 99 percent perspiration."
THOMAS EDISON
inventor of the phonograph, the motion picture camera,
and the practical lightbulb, and pioneer of electric power

'm an entrepreneur. A successful one.

But don't let that fool you.

I'm unqualified to be in any of my ventures.

If I was an employer and was handed my résumé, I wouldn't hire me.

I'm in KISS, currently celebrating our fortieth year of World Domination. I cofounded the band with my partner Paul Stanley. (Remember the word *partner*. It's going to come up a few times in this book.) KISS has broken box-office records set by Elvis and the Beatles. And we have literally thousands of licensed and merchandised products around the world that bear our name and likeness. From KISS Hello Kitty, to the KISS indoor golf course in Las Vegas, where everything glows in the dark under black light. It sits right across the street from the Hard Rock Hotel, and is always packed. You can get married there at the Hotter Than Hell Wedding Chapel, too. One of the unique events was when a nudist colony took over the place. Naked KISS golfing. What else?

KISS has gone where no band has gone before. And it doesn't look like it's going to slow down anytime soon. In fact, it just keeps getting bigger and bigger. We are everywhere.

In music licensing and merchandising, KISS is a juggernaut. There's not another group whose reach comes even close.

And that's not counting the albums and the T-shirts and the concert tours.

By some marketing estimates, the faces are the four most recognized faces on earth. I touched on this earlier—that our faces are registered trademarks. Let me prove it to you: Sweden is a monarchy. Do you know what the king and queen of Sweden look like? If you're not from Sweden, and especially if you're from America, there's a good chance you do not. If you are from there, of course, you know your own monarchs. But, whether or not you are from Sweden, I would wager that you've seen the KISS imagery. Even if you've never heard a song—even if we're just "that one band," you've seen that face somewhere before. This is what creating an icon means—a cultural icon defies the boundaries of state, nation, and language, class, taste, and tradition. If it's iconic, it is inescapable. We have made our face paint, our personas, inescapable.

My qualifications to be in KISS? None. I had no guidelines and no reference points. I had to invent myself, out of thin air. I played in a few high school bands doing cover songs. But before KISS, I had zero experience playing in a rock band that wears makeup. "How to Become a Rock Star" and "How to Build an Iconic image" are not taught in any school. And while I have written a few hundred songs, both for KISS and for other recording artists, I can't read or write musical notation. I can play guitar and bass and a bit of keyboards and drums, but as I said earlier, I never took lessons. My schooling in music theory? None. I am self-taught on every instrument I play, and I play completely by ear. I just do it.

KISS released their first album in 1974—long before cell phones, computers, MTV, Twitter, and Facebook—and rocketed to the top of the music industry. Within a year and a half of our formation, we were headlining Anaheim Stadium in California.

I have produced records for a number of other rock bands and artists. My résumé and experience as a producer before I decided to become one? None.

I launched my own record company, Simmons Records, originally partnered with RCA/BMG, later with Sanctuary Music, and most recently with Universal Canada. My experience in starting and running a record company? None.

I was Liza Minnelli's manager, to start, and I went on to manage other artists.

My experience and qualification to be a manager: None.

I have acted in motion pictures and on TV. In movies, I've had costarring and character roles in *Runaway* with Tom Selleck, *Wanted Dead or Alive* with Rutger Hauer, *Red Surf* with George Clooney, *Never Too Young to Die*, *The New Guy*, Mike Judge's *Extract* alongside Jason Bateman, Mila Kunis, Kristen Wiig, and Ben Affleck, and I recently finished appearing with Al Pacino in *Imagined*.

I have acted on numerous TV shows, including NBC's *Third Watch* and *Miami Vice*, and ABC's *Ugly Betty*.

My dramatic background before taking my first film role? None.

I coproduced the New Line film *Detroit Rock City* with Barry Levine, and created the cartoon show *My Dad the Rock Star* for Nickelodeon and *Mr. Romance* for Oxygen. Through the Gene Simmons Company, I've coproduced the TV shows *Gene Simmons Family Jewels*, which lasted for eight seasons and 167 episodes on A&E, and *Gene Simmons Rock School*, which ran for two seasons on VH1. Both shows were seen around the world.

My background in producing and creating TV shows and motion pictures before I decided to do it? None.

I was a cofounding partner in Cool Springs Life. It's a life equity strategy entity that loans high-net-worth individuals as much as $300 million at flat LIBOR plus a small bank fee. (LIBOR, or London Interbank Offered Rate, is the reduced interest rate that banks use when moving large chunks of money between themselves.) My partners in Cool Springs Life were Sam Watson, Rich Abramson, Simon Baitler, Bill Randolph, and Dave Carpenter, the former CEO of Transamerica, which at one point was the world's largest insurance company.

I designed the Cool Springs Life logo. When our public relations company told me that they didn't think the cable news stations would give coverage to a brand-new financial entity, I fired them and called up CNN, Fox, MSNBC, and Bloomberg myself to get my partner Sam Watson and me on television to promote it. Do it yourself.

My prior qualifications for creating a life equity strategy? None.

I was a cofounding partner, with David Lucatch and Rich Abramson, in Ortsbo, one of the largest universal language translators. I helped design the Ortsbo logo, and did marketing outreach (with Rich Abramson) and appeared at live events to promote it.

My track record in the technology industry? None.

I cofounded Simmons/Abramson Marketing with my then partner Rich Abramson. We had a grand total of one staff member, and we never had an office and therefore never paid rent. We were the marketing company for the Indy Racing League, as well as the Indianapolis 500. I created the "I Am Indy" marketing campaign and cowrote the Indy anthem of the same title with Bag, an artist who was signed to my Simmons Records label. And I forced the Indy Racing League to stop calling themselves IRL and simply call themselves IndyCar. My campaign lasted for several years, and was copied by the National Football League ("I Am the NFL"), by charities ("I Am CARE"), by radio stations ("I Am KROQ"), by clothing companies ("I Am Wolverine"), and even pet food manufacturers ("I Am IAMS").

My background in marketing? Well, in this instance, I would have to say that my experience with KISS gave me a grounding in marketing and spreading a brand that has served me well ever since. But I didn't know anything about IndyCar. I just had my gut, and that seemed to be all I needed.

I knew I could do anything. People told me I couldn't, because "you're just a musician." Well, I was, until I wasn't. Every CEO starts out without any qualifications. Then they jump in the deep end, and start swimming. It's the way I've always lived. It doesn't matter the task—if you're not qualified, you can become qualified. If you have never done it before, you can do it a first time. And then a second time. You can do it. Because I did.

Several years ago, I was honored to meet Frank Stronach, a very interesting gentleman who founded the massively successful auto parts company Magna International. Today, I'm proud to say that I'm a partner in the Stronach Group, which owns most of North America's major horse-racing tracks, including Santa Anita Park, Gulfstream Park, and Pimlico.

I had no title within the Stronach Group, and I couldn't tell you much about horses or jockeys. But I love horse racing.

I also noticed that horse racing was widely referred to as "the sport of kings." I did some research and determined that no one owned that phrase. So I quietly trademarked it, and now the Stronach Group owns the phrase The Sport of Kings™. I created an entire licensing and merchandising program, including logos, designs, hats, and T-shirts, and I connected Live Nation to mount live music festivals on Stronach Group racetracks.

My prior knowledge of horse racing? You guessed it. None.

I am a founding partner in Rock & Brews restaurants. My partners (there's that word again) are Michael Zislis, Dave Furano, and Dell Furano. Great food. Many choices of craft beers. Gluten-free pizzas and beers if you so desire. Restaurant brands usually take a long time to get traction. Not ours. We hit the ground running almost two years ago, and within a few months we wound up on the cover of *Franchise Times*.

Rock & Brews is growing by leaps and bounds. We have restaurants in Cabo, Mexico, on Maui, Hawaii, and in El Segundo and Redondo Beach, California. We have another site in the Delta terminal at Los Angeles International Airport, and one opening in Kansas City soon.

My schooling and experience for this business? None. I don't even cook.

I published my own magazine, called *Gene Simmons Tongue*, which lasted for five issues. It was published by Sterling/Macfadden. My partner was Allen Tuller. Hugh Hefner gave us an exclusive cover story for the first issue, and I interviewed Sir Richard Branson, Marvel Comics' Avi Arad, and the great Snoop Dogg (who was kind enough to wear an inverted version of my KISS makeup for the interview).

My schooling as a magazine publisher/editor? None.

Simmons Books was a co-venture with Michael Viner's Phoenix Books. Mostly, it was a way for me to write and publish my own books. I had always been interested in stories that resonate today, but have a long historical backdrop. Like, the oldest profession in the world. It's referenced in the New Testament with Mary Magdalene, and Mata Hari and the courtesans of Europe's Renaissance, the geishas of Japan, all the way to the Wall Street and

Hollywood call girls of today. Despite what the subject matter might imply, I approached my book with a historical, nonjudgmental approach. If you can get your hands on a copy, you may enjoy reading it. It became a *Los Angeles Times* bestseller.

My experience? Minimal. When I was fourteen years old, I used to self-publish my own magazines from home. I wrote, edited, and produced the zines via mimeograph, Rexograph, and eventually photocopy machines.

In 1999, I coproduced the motion picture *Detroit Rock City* for New Line Cinema. My partners were Barry Levine and Christine Haas.

I'd been trying since 1977 to get a KISS movie made. When I was growing up, I used the Beatles as my template for what I wanted to achieve. And the Beatles didn't just make records, they made movies—and good ones at that. But—aside from a lovably campy, made-for-TV movie we'd done in the seventies called *KISS Meets the Phantom of the Park*—getting a KISS movie made was easier said than done. Agencies couldn't make it happen. Managers couldn't make it happen. But I pushed forward, anyway. Eventually, a script called *Detroit Rock City*—about four teenagers who try to scam their way into a KISS concert—came into my hands from Barry Levine (whom you may remember from elsewhere in this book as our rock photographer; Barry would soon try his hand at making movies, and went on to make many including *Oblivion* with Tom Cruise and *Hercules* with The Rock). Before long, it was set up at New Line Cinema. Written and directed by Adam Rifkin, the movie featured almost everyone we knew, including Shannon. Although it was a KISS movie, we actually didn't appear in the movie till the very end.

However, behind any single success are a multitude of stillborn or endlessly delayed ventures. I had twenty other movie projects being developed around this time, but I failed to mount them.

I had the story of Casablanca Records head Neil Bogart at Paramount, with the Bogart family as partners. It was never made, though as of this writing, it is now finally a "go" picture with Justin Timberlake as Bogart. Originally, Mike Myers had been set to star.

My schooling to become a movie producer? None.

My experience? Minuscule.

My qualifications? Minimal.

And these are just two of many. It doesn't matter that I failed, a million times over. The only reason I was successful at anything was this same mentality—I jumped into the deep end, qualifications and naysayers be damned. You have to believe this about yourself. I'll go into this more later.

I am cofounding partner in LA KISS, our Los Angeles arena football team, after our manager, Doc McGhee, and AFL veteran Brett Bouchy started talking about KISS doing some cross-promotion with the AFL (Arena Football League). One thing led to another, and before long, Paul and I were offered a chance to buy into the team, along with Doc and Brett. We jumped at the chance. Doc suggested we call the team LA KISS. And Paul designed the logo.

I have done about fifty speaking engagements around the world, under my brand, Gene Simmons Rich & Famous Expos™. I own the trademark.

The reason I've always wanted to speak to people is that the education I received in public schools didn't prepare me for what life was really like, and, more specific, how I was going to pay my rent. I wanted to connect with people, share my experiences, and show them how they could improve their lives immediately. And in some cases, how a few of them might become ultrarich. It has happened, more than once.

I had initially wanted Creative Artists Agency to book me on speaking engagements, but I was told that my speaking fees could only fetch around $15,000 to $25,000. I didn't agree with that assessment, so I decided to book the speaking engagements myself.

So I spread the news. It didn't cost me a dime, and I never hired a PR agency or manager or booking agent to do so. I simply mentioned it when I did interviews on TV or radio, and presto, my first speaking engagement was offered. They made an offer, I countered, and we settled on $100,000. Since then, that's been my minimum speaking fee.

Multiply that by 50, and you will see why professionals can't always help you where you want to go.

Incidentally, handling things myself is something that I invariably wind up doing. If you want something done right, do it yourself. I didn't come up with that phrase, but I do live by it. The first time you try to do something yourself, it will—admittedly—be very difficult. As you gain success and traction, and you prove yourself on the battlegrounds, people will trust your ability to sell. At my level, doing things yourself is simply easier. And if you're committed to being your own boss, it's preferable.

Speaking engagements come at me from all directions, but hardly ever from a talent agency. Corporations usually contact me directly. And what I do is a hybrid autobiographical and hopefully inspirational and motivational speech. I never step up there with notes and I am never prepared. I simply start talking. By judging the makeup of the audience, I can steer my talking points and hopefully some of them will "get it." "Getting it" has to do with a mind-set: the idea that you can do almost anything, given the right place, the right time and the right thing. And plain old hard work. This is the reason I don't use notes—because I didn't use notes in my career. Sink or swim, you have to jump into the deep end. If you wait until you are ready, as the saying goes, you will wait forever.

It's one of the reasons I'm writing this book, and not someone else. There are acting teachers who don't know how to act, but they will tell you what you're doing wrong. There are football coaches who will tell you what you're doing wrong in football, although they may actually never play football. I'm a hybrid. I'm in front of the camera. And I'm in back of the camera. I'm onstage. And I'm backstage. I work in business, and I have a sense of the structure of business. Not all businesses, mind you. No one has that.

But I've cultivated enough business common sense to be able to apply it, and—make money.

My point in recounting all of these endeavors is that you shouldn't be afraid to try your hand at different things. You may need good partners—good writers, good production companies, investors, and stakeholders who can fill in the gaps of missing knowledge and experience—to help you get your venture off the ground.

But don't let the fear of failure keep you from trying in the first place. Most baseball swings sound like this: "Swoosh." But, if you swing enough, you *will* hit some of the balls.

10

Gene Simmons Family Jewels

"Life is what happens to you while you're busy making other plans."
JOHN LENNON
singer, songwriter, and Beatle

*G*ene Simmons Family Jewels lasted 167 episodes and seven seasons on the A&E network. (*I Love Lucy*, generally considered one of the greatest and most successful TV shows of all time, lasted 145 episodes.) We began shooting in 2006 and finished in 2011. We were seen around the world, in eighty-four countries. You can still watch us in reruns everywhere from South Africa to Bulgaria.

Since doing the show, Leslie Greif, the executive producer, has become a major force in television. His *Hatfields & McCoys* miniseries won three Emmy Awards.

I approached Leslie with the idea of doing a TV special that would show me recording and promoting my solo album. And Greif could also bring a camera crew with KISS as we finally went back on tour to Australia and New Zealand. We also filmed at my home, as I prepared to launch the album with a party at the Key Club in Los Angeles.

At home, the cameras were introduced to Sophie, Nick, and Shannon. Although it wasn't planned, the camera immediately fell in love with them. When my family was on camera, I became yesterday's news.

A&E liked the TV special—titled *24/7*, in reference to my work ethic—and it did well when it was broadcast, so the network approached me about doing a reality series, although that phrase meant nothing to me at the time. The proposed series would focus on my business ventures and my family. I had never planned for this, and would have never imagined that all of us would ever be interesting enough for public consumption. But there it was, plain as day.

I also never imagined that the show would turn out to be a real diary of my family. Its ups and its downs. Its family values. Although I had never visited a shrink, the show wound up showing me a real reflection of myself. I had always known who I was, but I had never had to confront that person before.

There were great times. There were funny times. And there were some very sad and hurtful times. We traveled around the world. To England. Europe. South America. Canada. We traveled to Africa, where for the first time I met the children I had been financially supporting for twenty-five years in Zambia through the organization ChildFund.

By the time the show was nearing its seventh season, Nick and Sophie were almost grown up, and it became clear that Shannon was finally getting a clear picture of who I was and what I had been—partly through the show.

It was all there, plainly represented on television screens around the world. It was embarrassing. I was ashamed. And I had it coming.

For many years, I had been selfish, arrogant, and delusional about all sorts of things. That same delusional faith in myself that helped me get things done in the business world became a double-edged sword, and put a strain on my relationships with my family. I deluded myself into thinking I could do whatever I wanted outside of our home and family, and that it would never get back to the family or hurt them. I was an idiot.

Shannon was going to leave me because of my ways. I had been unfaithful. I was constantly touring, constantly working. Shannon stayed home and raised the kids. She drove them to school and back every day. She became the school's lunch president, and negotiated and oversaw the lunch program. In fact, she was there every day, serving lunch to every child in school, so she could keep a close eye on Nick and Sophie. She hovered over them every day to make sure they became ethical, moral human beings. In point of fact, Shannon raised the kids. I just worked.

When things began to leak, we sat down and talked about whether we wanted to be honest with our viewers, and show ourselves as we were, or if we wanted to keep it lighthearted—the safe route, we thought, to keep the show going. We decided that we wanted to show all of it on the series, no matter the consequences. Shannon had had enough fakery in her life—if she was going to be part of a reality show, she wanted to show something truly real, as it was happening. My wandering eye. Shannon's commitment to the kids. My facelift. Shannon's heartbreak, when it dawned on her that I had been unfaithful for so many years. We showed my shame. We showed real pain and emotion when Shannon broke down. We filmed Shannon and I going to marriage counselors to try to address my issues. And for some time, Shannon was going to leave me. Both Nick and Sophie were ashamed and hurt by their father: me.

It became clear to me that I was going to lose Shannon and the kids. And that I had to get over myself and finally grow up. Ever since I was a small child, perhaps because my father had left us, I convinced myself I would never get married. And that I would never answer to anyone. *Anyone.* Not my mother. Not Shannon.

Not anyone. I would do as I pleased, the rest of the world be damned.

If you watch the early episodes of our show, that part of me was clear. I wrote books on the subject. If you read my previous autobiography, or my other books, you'll see a different guy, with different views on this topic. I did interviews on the subject. I went on *Oprah* and *The View* and espoused my antimarriage philosophies. And my selfish philosophies. Every time, it hurt Shannon and the kids. And I didn't care. Delusionally and shamefully, I never thought about it.

But it was becoming clearer and clearer to me that the line in the sand had been drawn, and that I would have to do some fast growing up, or risk throwing it all away. And, because Shannon had too much integrity to lie to the world about it, we decided to film all of that. If the tabloids wanted to talk, we were going to show them first.

I decided to do some real self-analysis. The show arranged for a Marriage Boot Camp. It consisted of a few couples with real issues. The difference was that they were all married and were trying to save their marriages. Shannon and I were never married, and we were trying to figure out how to save our relationship.

One of the exercises, though I was never told about it when I walked into the room, was "What would be the last things I say to my beloved, as she lay in her coffin?" I walked into a room filled with all the other couples, and there was Shannon, lying in a coffin. They asked me to walk up to her, as if she were dead, and talk to her.

It almost seems comical, written out like this. But at the time it was more than I could bear. And it made me really confront my shortcomings. My selfishness. My arrogance. And I was heartbroken at all the pain and suffering I had caused.

We went to Belize. On an idyllic beach, I dropped to my knee and looked up to the person who had stuck by me for twenty-eight years, without ever asking or demanding anything. I tearfully asked Shannon if she would consider marrying a man who was clearly not worthy of her love.

Shannon was in tears, clearly hurt by it all. She was confused, but miraculously said yes.

But the pain and suffering I had brought on Shannon wasn't over. We had lived together for twenty-eight years with a cohabitation agreement that we had both signed with individual counsel. I was always afraid of the cliché of clichés—that women only want you for your money. Shameful as that may sound, it was true.

Before we got married, I also asked if Shannon would mind doing a prenup, with both of us having our own counsel. That brought on more pain and suffering to Shannon, as each of our lawyers was whispering into our ears about how we had each sacrificed so much, and how the other one should not get what they were asking for. I suppose that's what your lawyer is supposed to do. But your beloved only winds up getting hurt even more.

We had almost broken up on more than one occasion over the prenup negotiations, but thankfully, they were finally over.

Our wedding date was set, on October 1, 2011—twenty-eight and a half years after we began living together.

The wedding was at the Beverly Hills Hotel.

It was a perfect wedding. It was a beautiful, sunshiny day. Friends and family all were there, as were the other members of KISS: Paul, Tommy, and Eric. So was our dog Snippy. No one threw up. No one passed out. Shannon wrote out her vows and so did I. In front of all the invited guests, I heard Shannon's beautiful words to me. I was going to read my vows, but then decided to crumple up the paper and just speak from my heart. I told her that

I was deeply in love with her. And that she had been the only true love of my life. And that I have a lot to make up for, all the pain and suffering I had caused her and the kids, and that I would do so for the rest of my life.

We kissed, for the first time as husband and wife.

And then the party began. It lasted well into the night. We had a ten-piece big band, fronted by Brenna Whitaker, who rocked it all night. Then KISS got up and played a few songs. And then Nick and Sophie got up and sang a few songs. And then Shannon—surprise—got up and sang in her beautiful voice.

As I write this, we've been together more than thirty years. And we have been married to each other for over a year and a half.

Now that the show has stopped filming and I have some distance from it, I believe that our show helped me to confront myself about all sorts of things. As silly as it may sound, that damn reality show actually dug deep. My family. My shortcomings. Our show was also a diary of our kids and our family growing up together. When we first started shooting, Nick and Sophie were preteens. By the time we had finished, they were adults. And Shannon was more beautiful than ever. She still is.

And I'm proud to say she's my wife.

They say reality shows break up families.

In our case, *Gene Simmons Family Jewels* forced me to come clean, with the family and with myself.

Gene Simmons Family Jewels saved our family.

The lesson, for business and for life, is to keep your priorities straight. If you come across a zero-sum situation in a business endeavor, you must recognize what you simply cannot live without. I was made to pick from two available paths, and when faced with that, I had to go with the path that led to Shannon. So it is with business—when you take the world by the collar, you must understand why you are doing so. You have to know why it's worth it. And when you come to a fork in the road, you must keep your eye trained on what is most important to you—whatever that happens to be. Your decision will become clear if you can do this well enough.

11

Philanthropy/Giving Back

Once you make that Big Money and you succeed at climbing the ladder of success, I want to instill in you a quality that needs to be there—and one that you may be surprised to hear me endorse: *giving back*.

Take your money and create new jobs. Take your money and invest in starting new ventures, which creates more jobs, and enables capitalism to keep on working on its own, without depending on handouts from the government. Government, as you may well have guessed by now, means well, but it doesn't really know how to create jobs. And that's because government is run by politicians, instead of businessmen and -women. That should speak for itself.

The above may suggest I support the idea of *charity*, as we have come to know it. But I do not.

If someone is on their last monthly rent, and they're about to be thrown out of their home, then yes. Loan them some money, so they can go out, get a job, and afford to keep paying rent. Notice I said "loan" them some money. The reason for that is that I believe charity makes the recipient feel beholden. A loan, on the other hand, allows the recipient to maintain a degree of self-respect. Especially when and if they can afford to pay the loan back.

Personally, I have some concerns with some of our generally accepted ideas about charity, although I do a lot of philanthropic work myself. I'm proud that America's capitalist system has allowed me to do well enough in life so that I can give something back.

I haven't called a press conference or issued a press release to announce to the world what a good guy I am, but perhaps it is time I do, so that others can do the same. It's probably the only thing I *haven't* bragged about extensively—I certainly love bragging about everything else.

As I mentioned before, I support children, twelve hundred of them, in Zimbabwe in southern Africa. I initially did this through ChildFund (formerly Christian Children's Fund), and now do it on my own. Most of these children had nothing and often go to sleep hungry. That will never happen again, if I can help it. I feed and clothe them, and buy books for them, but *only* if they attend school. At the school, they're fed decent, fresh, hot meals.

While we were in Zambia filming an episode of *Gene Simmons Family Jewels*, we were having breakfast at a hotel when Shannon pointed out a young guy who she said I should meet. Brendan Clark, it turned out, was twenty-seven and was from Perth, Australia. He had just gotten married and had his mother there with him. He was in Zambia on a humanitarian mission: he wanted to make a difference.

Although I had been doing charity work in Africa through ChildFund for decades, I decided to join Brendan in doing charity work that directly improved children's lives—I always like the direct approach, and the "do it yourself" approach. I paid for a young girl's college education and paid to build a young man's family a home.

Brendan and I fund a food program that feeds more than one thousand Zambian children at school. The food is bought fresh daily and trucked to the schools. It is cooked and prepared at the schools (the reason the food has to be trucked in, incidentally, is that there are bandits who would rob the stockpiles if they were kept at the school overnight).

The only hope of escaping poverty is education. If a child is willing to attend school—and sometimes that means walking ten miles on bare feet to school—there will be a fresh, hot meal waiting. Often, it's the only meal the child will eat that day. Parents attend as well.

The look of joy on a child's face, enjoying a hot meal, is humbling beyond anything I could put into words. If that sounds a little bit like the boy you met in the first chapter, that's because it is. The narrative is circular.

We also purchased some ambulances, which we had shipped from Perth to Zambia. The ambulances are literally hospitals on wheels. They go to people in need, instead of assuming that people have the means to walk miles to a hospital, or have the money to pay for treatment.

The real-life lesson for me here is that, although I take great personal pride in dreaming big and achieving big, the biggest achievement of all is to be able to help another human being. I know this sounds like I'm trying to convince you how great I am. And usually, I do like talking about how great I am. But whether or not you like me, or think I'm a braggart, not everyone is fortunate enough to be born in America and enjoy the benefits it provides. I know that well. Children living in countries like Zambia typically don't even own a pair of shoes, and sometimes eat nothing the entire day. The infrastructure in those countries is barebones, and the lack of health care is shocking. I'm not running for Miss America. I'm not asking you to think of me as charitable, or as a good person, and I'm not trying to bombard you with clichés. Pretend it's not me telling you this—pretend it's someone else. I'm being straight with you—if you have any success in this life, you don't have the right *not* to help someone else. Dying with the most money will bring you a certain level of satisfaction—but you will forever be denied the full measure of your satisfaction as a successful *human being* if you do not embark on charitable ventures like this. Your empire of dirt won't have any reason to stand.

I sleep better at night, knowing I have made a small difference in children's lives.

I also do work for the Wounded Warrior Project, and helped to raise millions of dollars for our volunteer military. And I continue to work on behalf of our men and women in uniform.

I have helped to raise millions for the Elizabeth Glaser Pediatric AIDS Foundation. It breaks my heart when a child is born with hardships it had no hand in creating. On my guest stints on the TV game show *Are You Smarter Than A Fifth Grader?*, I won $500,000 and donated all of it to the foundation.

I have helped Shannon and Sophie raise millions for SickKids Hospital in Toronto. And Sophie started her own charity, called Sophie's Place, in Vancouver, which treats thousands of abused children every year. A second Sophie's Place is about to open.

There are many more examples, but I'm sure that you get the idea.

Mostly, I make an effort to give to those who have no other option.

I'm in favor of giving people a sense of self-determination, and not letting them feel as if they owe anyone anything. Charity is a wonderful thing, if you can do it.

However, some charity organizations are also a quicksand of corruption. Running a business is fine. Pretending you are doing it for charitable reasons, when really you are profiting immensely from abusing people's empathy, is another thing entirely.

Don't give people fish. Teach them how to fish for themselves, for the sake of sustainability.

The welfare system, in my estimation, should be based on simple tasks that would pay recipients for the work they do, instead of simply handing funds out for free. Clean up the graffiti in your neighborhood. Clean up the garbage in your neighborhood. Be a good neighbor. Report any suspicious, potential criminal activity in your neighborhood to the police. And get paid for it.

Not handouts.

Work.

Give a person dignity. Let them feel that they've *earned* the money they got.

Every Christmas, we all run around buying gifts for everyone. Which is terrific. Christmas is a great time of giving, and we are blessed to be able to do so. We buy all sorts of gifts for family members and friends, as well as for people we barely know. How many of those gifts wind up in piles shoved into closets and quickly forgotten?

I stopped doing all of that almost ten years ago. Now, every year, I send a card to everyone on my Christmas list. The card says something along the lines of "I have made a donation in your name to help change someone's life dramatically. Please go to sleep tonight knowing that you have helped to make the world a better place." And, yes, as you may have concluded by now, I guilt people into giving back. The social awkwardness of pressuring someone to do the right thing is worth the result. If someone as selfish as I am feels obligated to do these things, you must do them, too. It's not a choice—it is an obligation. You must give back.

I also send cash to Kiva (kiva.org) in other people's names. Kiva is a micro bank with a very practical and effective charitable model. It makes interest-free loans, some as small as $25, to people living in Africa, Southeast Asia, and other places of need. For example, a $1,000 loan to a single mother living close to the Kalahari Desert in Africa means that she can afford to buy a few cows and dig a well for water. Overnight, her world is changed. She can feed her children, and earn a little bit selling milk to her neighbors. It also means her small village will now have water.

Once she pays back the loan, Kiva loans out that amount to another family in need. In that way, it's a gift that keeps on giving.

I wish our government system functioned more like Kiva and other micro banks.

Many of us, in this age of entitlement, look to the government to do all sorts of things for us. I contend that we should be able to do for ourselves.

One of the real benefits of making Big Money is that you can be philanthropic and create new jobs for people. The problem you ultimately want to have, as an entrepreneur, is deciding who to help, not deciding who can help you. Work your way to this level. And when you do, fulfill your obligation.

Before I ever had success, I was motivated by selfish motives. I wanted to become successful and make lots of money. I could then buy my mother a house and give myself a better lifestyle. Mostly though, I was motivated to become successful as a goal. Once I achieved what people consider "wealth," humanitarian notions simply came at me, big and strong. Not everyone in the world is as fortunate, or lives in a luxurious country like America.

So, in my late twenties, I started to contribute to charities. And, so did the band. It made me feel good. I thought of that very first CARE package we received so long ago in Israel, with the can of peaches, and the torn sweater and the American children's books with Bugs Bunny. It was time to give back.

Of course, my story isn't unique. The most successful entre-preneurs give to charities, start foundations, fund scholarships, and so on. And what you'll find, if you work hard enough, are at the right place at the right time with the right thing and end up wealthy, is that you, too, will want to give back.

Wealth for its own sake is an empty shell. Wealth that includes making other people's lives better will reward you even more than the beautiful mansion you live in. It does for me. It will for you. And, like me, your charity may inspire yet another entrepreneur to rise up.

This book is about how to be successful. I will tell you that I was not truly successful until I decided to also be charitable.

PART II

YOU

12

Who Are You?

"Build your own dreams, or someone else will hire you to build THEIRS."
FARRAH GRAY
businessman, investor, philanthropist, author, and motivational speaker

Where did I learn what I know? How did I become me? Did school and college prepare me for the real world? I went through the school system and graduated from college with a bachelor of arts in education degree that qualified me to teach, or write books. But did all that prepare me for how I made the Big Money? No.

And I suspect the same is true with you. Unless you took courses in architecture, engineering, or pre-med, the rest of your liberal arts education hardly prepares you for life as the business warrior and champion you envision yourself to be.

Oh, you'll be the hit of the cocktail party with your liberal arts college degree. You'll be able to quote Kant and Kierkegaard, and there's nothing wrong with that. But you won't be able to pay off your car loan or your first home mortgage with that information.

In other words, grade school education, high school education, and liberal arts college degrees generally won't prepare you for how you're going to make a living, let alone how you're going to make the Big Money.

You'll notice that I keep using the term *Big Money*. That's because none of us (including yours truly) wants to *just* make money. We all want to make BIG Money.

You *can* go to a "directional" education program, that is, study to be an architect, or a dentist, or a lawyer. Those degrees will certainly help you earn a living, but they'll cost a lot of money and take many more years of study.

What I'm about to tell you is not politically correct. In fact, it may come as a shock to you. But here it is: you don't need a lot of systemized education to achieve great things *and* make lots of money.

Education *is* important, and I urge you to get one. But if you can't afford to go to college or vocational school, it's important to understand what the word *entrepreneur* means.

Merriam-Webster defines *entrepreneur* as "one who organizes, manages, and assumes the risks of a business or enterprise." What being an entrepreneur means is that you have to think and do for yourself.

It is important to keep this phrase in mind: "You have an inferred fiduciary duty to yourself." It means that it's up to YOU.

It's up to you to educate yourself outside school. It's up to you to make friends with people who are more successful than you are. Respectfully, get rid of your chip-dippin', TV-watchin', happy-with-my-life, don't-wanna-do-anything-else friends. They won't help you. Surround yourself with people who are more successful than yourself.

It's up to you what you do with your free time. Do you goof around and take vacations, or do nothing after work? Do you do nothing on your weekends? Do you go to ball games or bars with your drinking buddies? Get rid of those guys immediately. They won't help you.

Or do you spend your evenings and leisure time devoted

to YOU? To your dreams. To your aspirations. To making Big Money.

Does your significant other ask, "What's more important, me or your career?" If he or she uses that line on you, you may want to be honest and say, "It's my career first, and then you. Without earning a good living, I can't provide us both with the life we want."

If that doesn't resonate with them, you may want to consider dumping that person from your life. They may be the biggest psychological hurdle in your quest for the Big Money.

I'm sorry, but that's the truth. You can't have it both ways.

There have been books written about the "10,000-hour rule," which claims that the key to becoming a success in any field is getting 10,000 hours of experience in what you want to be successful at, or the theory that you need to put in that much time to become any good at something. As it happens, the Beatles spent 10,000 hours playing together in clubs in Germany in the early sixties before starting their recording career, and Bill Gates spent that amount of time programming his high school's computers in 1968.

You can't devote equal amounts of time to your beloved girlfriend/boyfriend/husband/wife *and* your career. If you want to succeed faster and bigger, you will have to choose YOU first, then everyone else. Or, as I like to put it, ME!!!

Be selfish. Be committed to yourself *first*.

Remember, YOU first.

Girlfriend/boyfriend/wife/husband/friends *second*.

The giving back comes later.

An important point to remember: no matter what you read, and no matter what anyone tells you, there is no such thing as "the Ten Secret Rules for Becoming Enormously Rich." If it were that simple, then everyone would be rich already.

The journey that you must make to become a real estate mogul and have your name become a brand, like Lefrak or Trump, is not the same road that a comic-book geek (and I am one) has to travel to launch his comic book company (like my Simmons Comics) and get production companies to develop his comic-book creations into TV shows and films.

So what does all of this mean? It means YOU will have to figure it out for yourself.

That's what *entrepreneur* really means.

YOU make up your own rules. And YOU have to educate yourself and learn whatever you need to learn to have the tools to go out there and be the business warrior and champion that's inside you, yearning to get out.

They don't teach that stuff in school.

The reason this book is called *ME, Inc.* is that I AM THE MOST IMPORTANT PERSON IN MY PRIVATE AND BUSINESS LIFE.

That's right, ME first. Maybe it's not politically correct, but it's necessary, if you want to increase your chances of success big-time.

Take a hint from the airline industry. If there is turbulence on your flight, the crew will tell you to take the life-sustaining oxygen mask that just fell in front of your face and put it on YOUR face first. Not your child's face. On the surface, it sounds cruel, but it makes pragmatic sense, because if you can't help yourself *first*, you will not be able to help anyone else. Not your child, not your family, not your friends, not anyone.

To some extent, capitalism in America has its hands tied behind its back. But there is still enough of a capitalist business world out there that will give you a chance of making Big Money.

In point of fact, you cannot fail. Yes, you heard me right. YOU CANNOT FAIL.

You have everything to gain, and little or nothing to lose, by throwing yourself headfirst into your entrepreneurial endeavor. If your business fails and you cannot pay off your debts, under current business laws you can declare Chapter 7 or Chapter 11, which means that with a decent lawyer, you will be forgiven all your debts and you can start all over again. Of course, because you're an ethical person, as soon as you hit the big time, you will pay off your debts anyway, even though you may not be legally required to do so.

The only thing holding you back from succeeding in America may be YOU.

Before you undertake this journey, you must have the heart of a lion and your self-esteem must be intact. If your self-esteem isn't strong, then bluff and *act* like it's strong. Grit your teeth and *pretend* that you have enormous self-confidence. Fake it until you make it.

If a bully comes up to you, do not show weakness. It will make it easier for him to beat you up. If you show enormous self-confidence and show no fear, the bully may, just may, back off. A small chance at greatness is better than giving up.

In the wild, if faced with a wolf that's about to attack, your best chance for survival is to stand your ground, puff out your chest as large as it can go, wildly flail your arms in the air, make a lot of noise, and *always* look straight into the eyes of the predator. If you do that, you may survive. In other words, you will win.

The same principle applies in business transactions, though of course, the loan application and your proposal count, as does your demeanor. When you sit with a bank or financial official, and you're looking to get a loan for your business venture, be big. Be strong. Be confident (and make sure your idea is worth being confident about). Be all that you can be. If it doesn't come naturally, *fake it.*

Remember, no matter what your business proposal is, what they'll really be investing in is YOU.

That's why there are often key-man clauses in corporate contracts. What is Trump Enterprises worth without Donald Trump? What's Virgin worth without Sir Richard Branson? I know both of those men, and I can guarantee that even if they were completely unknown, when one of them walked into a room, you would *still* stop what you were doing and take notice.

Invariably, if a vacuum cleaner salesman rings your front door, he will be selling HIMSELF first. The vacuum cleaner is secondary. It always comes back to YOU, and it always will.

Say what you mean. Mean what you say. Let your word be your bond. Your reputation will precede you. You've heard this all before. The most important word here? You guessed it: YOU!

Remember, it's how you *feel* about your aspirations and dreams every day that is the most important thing, because these feelings will drive you to action.

It's your WILL to succeed, your never-ending COMMITMENT to yourself to succeed, your "never-take-no-for-an-answer" mind-set, and your PERSEVERANCE that will help you win and win big.

It's important to note that rock stars, politicians, and other people with position, power, and wealth weren't born that way.

They had to earn it.

They worked for it.

They had to make up their own rules.

They had to sell themselves first, before their product.

They had to educate themselves. School was over, and self-education began when they left school.

And they were willing to work harder than you to get there.

Do you have what it takes?

Will you let anyone or anything stop you from where you want to go?

Have you ever said something like "I just want enough to have a comfortable life"?

If you have, this is not the book for you. And you may not be an entrepreneur.

Unless you have incredible luck and win the lottery, you will not obtain riches with an "I just want enough to be comfortable" mind-set. Even if you do win the lottery, you will probably not know what to do with the money, and will soon be back where you started from, just like many lottery winners. They won big fortunes, and in a short time went bankrupt. Some got divorced, left their families, and even committed suicide. Google it if you don't believe me.

You have to have the guts and the will to do what our military urges: BE ALL THAT YOU CAN BE.

Go Big. Or Go Home.

You will notice, as you are reading this book, that I repeat things. A lot. As if I'm losing my memory in my old age.

Good.

It's intentional.

You and I and everyone else have the attention span of gnats. And that means that saying or doing anything once simply doesn't work. Never has. Never will.

Saying or doing anything should be like the chorus of the hit song. Before the song is through, you will have heard the chorus (the memorable part of the song) over and over again.

The repetition will make you remember the song and hum it to yourself long after the song is over.

"If at first you don't succeed (and you *won't*, believe me), try, try again."

That one is correct.

Even if you *do* succeed, try, try again.

Keep at it.

Do it over and over again.

Keep improving what you're doing.

Always.

THE ART OF MORE: PRINCIPLE #1

SELF-CONFIDENCE IS YOUR GREATEST BUSINESS PARTNER

The prime building block for popularity can be boiled down to one trait: self-confidence. It is neither genetic, inherent, nor for sale. But it is learnable and 100 percent essential to success. And the first step, even before you do your own due diligence (as you should), is to have an enormous, almost delusional sense of self-confidence.

LET ME REPEAT THAT: *AN ENORMOUS, ALMOST DELUSIONAL SENSE OF SELF-CONFIDENCE.*

You must learn to be able to stand in front of strangers, who couldn't care less about you, and convince them that what you have to offer is something they need and cannot do without. What you are offering is the greatest thing you could possibly have access to. What you are offering them is YOU!

13

You—The Me, Inc. Business Model

> "Anybody who can afford a box of business cards can afford a website. Any company with an 800 number can move its services to the Web for peanuts by comparison. The extreme case of corporate promotion is to strip away all other aspects of your business and sell goods or services via the Net alone, as Amazon.com has done with books."
>
> **NATHAN MYHRVOLD**
> inventor, entrepreneur, and former chief technology officer for Microsoft

> "Making money is art and working is art and good business is the best art."
>
> **ANDY WARHOL**
> pop-art innovator, visual artist, author, publisher, and filmmaker

What is your definition of "success"?

This book is about MONEY. It's called *Me, Inc.* because my attitude is this: better it's MY MONEY than anyone else's.

There's a very old platitude that goes "the love of money is the root of all evil." The person who came up with that statement was, in my view, severely misguided, and missing a large—perhaps the largest—source of crime in the world. The implication is that money, by its nature in having value at all, corrupts people simply by being valuable.

As I said in my book *Sex Money KISS*, it's the "lack of money that is actually the root of all evil" (I've since discovered that this quote has been attributed variously to Mark Twain or George Bernard Shaw). And, no, I don't mean "all"—I often use hyperbole, so you'll have to excuse that. There are exceptions to every rule, and the usual white-collar crime suspects you hear about are, of course, greedy and evil individuals. But this platitude, "money is the root of all evil," carries a lot of weight with people, and it's important to note that it does not take desperation into account. If I didn't have a dime, I might hold up a 7-Eleven for a loaf of bread, because I would be desperate enough to do so. But if I were worth $100 million, I would never think of doing that. The lack of money is why people hold up banks.

After you become successful, give it all away if you like—to your family, to your loved ones, to charity, whatever makes you happy. But before you have any money, you can't do squat.

The truth is that it's the lack of money that is the root of so much evil in the world. Crooks hold you up for money. And they tell us that the single biggest problem with relationships and marriages is money; even infidelity comes in second.

Money allowed me to make my mother's life easier. Money allowed me to buy her a house. And to buy her anything she wanted. Without money, I couldn't have done any of it.

And for those of you who might say, "Oh, but money can't make you happy," well, that's patently untrue. If you're a miserable son of a bitch, it's still better to be a *rich*, miserable son of a bitch.

When Scrooge is rehabilitated at the end of *A Christmas Carol*, he can do a lot of good and make people happy, because he's got money to do it with. A rehabilitated Scrooge *without* money wouldn't be in a position to help anyone much.

But lest we dwell too much on money, I want to make it clear that it is the love of labor and not the love of money that will give you rewards. There is a big difference between going to work and loving to work. It is important that you take this to heart.

And when you embark on this great personal journey you're going to go on, I would suggest you implement my Me, Inc. Business Model.

Ultimately, even if you are well educated, it is *still* up to you to figure out how to get a job, and how to make lots of money.

The answer is, Me, Inc.

YOU are the corporation.

YOU are the one who should form a limited liability company.

YOU are the one who will have to figure out how the capitalist model works. That's something that they don't teach the masses.

The future is here.

The future is now.

The old business model had to do with a workplace: a building or an office where everyone came to work. We're speaking of non-manufacturing entities. And we're not addressing farming.

The old way was expensive. As a company owner, you had to rent or buy a workplace. You had to rent or buy equipment—chairs, desks, computers, filing cabinets—storage facilities, parking, and all sorts of other items.

There were also many lost hours during the workday. A worker had to travel to and from work. Multiply all that travel time and cost by five days a week and fifty weeks a year, and you've got a lot of wasted time and money for one employee.

The new business model is simpler. And if you can apply it to your endeavor, it will save you a lot of money and a lot of wasted time (which also costs money). If you can, work at home. Save the time and money of commuting to and from work. And save the stress of commuting. Or if you're starting a company, you work from home and let the Internet do the rest for you.

The new, twenty-first-century streamlined company can rent a facility for a short time and refocus the business plan; then workers can go off to their respective homes to implement the program.

Working from home gives the worker a lot more flexibility and more usable hours to get the work done. Remember, anywhere from two to four hours a day are wasted on traveling to and from work.

And if you work at home, maybe you don't take a full hour off to eat. Maybe you only take half an hour.

And you can stop work at any time to do something else, as long as you finish the work.

The worker model of the twenty-first century is about going back to the basics: YOU are the boss. YOU make the rules. YOU, in essence, become the company.

But that also means YOU are responsible for getting the work done.

You may not realize it, but the Social Security system is a form of insurance. You pay "premiums" (a certain amount of money every month or every year) and later on, at "maturity," you get to access those funds, which come to you in weekly checks. The Social Security system is your insurance that you will still be able to survive after you can no longer work. There are different forms of retirement security, including an IRA (individual retirement account) or Roth IRA. I urge you to find out what all of that is. Google it. It's simple. Educate yourself.

Your job will often automatically deduct a certain amount for your IRA. That's good, because for the most part, you won't do it. Mostly, you live in the here and now. Mostly, you spend what you earn. Mostly, you don't save for a rainy day. Mostly, you think you will never grow old and won't have a problem being able to support yourself.

Mostly.

Farmers are often smarter in their business model than the masses who work in the corporate system. And that's because a farmer has only himself to depend on. If you work at a corporate entity, there is always the company there to pay your wages. Rain or shine. Always dependable, at least until the company becomes insolvent.

Back to the farmer: He knows when to plant the seeds. He knows how much it costs. He knows what the price of goods is. And he can approximate his profit margin if all things go as planned. Of course, one bad winter or one flood can change all that. So, in a very real way, for a farmer, it's feast or famine. Which is why he absolutely must have insurance of all kinds as a farmer.

In a corporate environment, insurance isn't necessarily the first thing on your mind.

But perhaps it should be.

Health insurance. Car insurance. Homeowner's insurance. All sorts of insurance. It's all worth considering. Do the research.

You don't want to sit and stare as your house goes up in flames, or your car is totaled in a wreck you had nothing to do with, and have no financial parachute.

Farmers are smarter than you are. They have to be.

A farmer will rarely plant only one kind of crop. He can't. If he only plants potatoes, and the price of potatoes takes a huge dip in the marketplace, he will be wiped out. So he plants different kinds of crops (get ready for a Wall Street investment term—"spread the risk").

This is the most basic form of *diversification*. Simply put, this means never putting all your eggs in one basket. If you drop the basket, all of the eggs shatter.

The same business model that a farmer uses is what's often recommended on Wall Street: Spread the risk. Invest in a few different things. Never just one.

A good piece of advice for all of you entering the corporate world.

Is what you do for a living the only thing you know how to do? If so, that's not good. What happens when that "thing" is no longer in demand? What's your fallback position? What else can you do?

Farmers also need to get along with their neighbors. It's important.

If a flood wipes out half of the farmer's crops, while his next-door neighbor is left untouched, he can hopefully count on his neighbor to help him out.

That's because the next time a tornado rips through the area, the neighbor might be hit and may need the farmer's help.

So, if you're a farmer, it makes good business sense to get along with your neighbor.

How about you? You sit in your corporate cubicle. Do you get along with the person in the next cubicle? Do you talk trash about them?

Remember, they may fly by you on the way up the ladder of success. Your "neighbor" might become your boss.

Work well with everyone.

Don't burn bridges. Don't trash-talk. Don't gossip. Not in the workplace. Not at home.

Find a hobby.

When you buy a hamburger, do you understand how much each meat patty costs McDonald's? How much do employees make? How much for the building's rent? How much for

YOU—THE ME, INC. BUSINESS MODEL **101**

insurance? How much does the McDonald's franchisee profit with each burger sold? If you wanted to be a McDonald's franchisee, it would be to your advantage to know all that.

Do you partner up, or do you use consultants? I highly recommend consultants or short-term employees. If you hire someone, it also means that you may need to fire them, and that can get difficult. In present-day America, unions can still go on strike and shut you down.

At home, *you* are the boss. It's your home, so if you invite someone to your home, they're allowed to stay. If you decide you've had enough of your invited guest, you can ask them to leave. And they have to. After all, it's *your* home.

But if you have a business—which is, after all, still your "work home," and which you paid for—you *invite* someone to come work for you. But in business, it's very difficult to ask them to leave. I find this astonishing.

There is also the idea that the employer has a responsibility to make sure you go on vacation two weeks every year and *still* get paid full wages, and that if you work overtime, the employer will have to pay you double and sometimes triple time per hour. The employer also has to pay for your health care, and your maternity leave. . . .

If you want to build a business in America using the *old* business model—that is, dealing with lots of employees, labor unions, etc.—the hurdles are nearly insurmountable. Instead, you can work with consultants, who get paid for the work they do, and can be fired or let go at any time, for just about any reason. Or set up your business in a "right to work" state—where unions don't hold sway, and where you are allowed to negotiate for your own wages without interference.

If you're reading this book, there's a choice you'll need to make. You can decide you just want to work for a living: pick up your paycheck every week, and have the union protect you (and your health care, your paid vacation, etc.) against the evil employer.

Or you can decide to become an entrepreneur. YOU will become the corporation. YOU will become the boss. YOU stand to make the big bucks. In order to do that, you cannot and should not build your venture on the old business model.

Remember, if you're building a business in America, YOU are the last person who will get paid (*if* there is any profit). The workers always get paid first. And their health coverage, retirement funds, and other issues are also paid first. Buildings, office space, rent, insurance, equipment—these things all cost lots of money, and *you* are the one who will pay for it all.

If, after all that money goes out, there is any profit left, you will still have to pay tax on that to the United States government. The 50 percent tax bracket kicks in, when you earn approximately $250,000 and over. So you'll wind up with *half* of that last precious dollar—*after* everyone else, and everything else, gets paid first: about $125,000.

Not much of an incentive to start a company in America, is it?

Which is why I want to stress the idea of ME, as a corporation.

Have a killer instinct. I still do. And I don't have to. I would, arguably, make a living without trying very hard at this point. My bills are paid. I don't have to write this book, or be in a rock band, or be partners in all the companies I've mentioned.

Why do it?

Because I'm a champion. I pride myself not only on what I've achieved, but on what I dream of achieving.

I refuse to sit on my thumb all day and talk about yesterday.

That's for wimps.

I'm a today and tomorrow person.

The past is wonderful, but it's the past. The only thing that counts is the here and now, and tomorrow.

Are you like me?

If you are, then you are greatly increasing your chances of becoming a proud member of the Me, Inc. mind-set.

YOU first.

Everyone else second.

THE ART OF MORE: PRINCIPLE #2

PAY YOUR DUES, DO THE WORK

It's a good practice, before making a major life decision regarding what you want to do to make money, to get your hands on everything that's out there. Put yourself out there and dive in. As far as I'm concerned, that's far braver than trying to be a trailblazer and waiting for the public to catch on. If life gives you an opportunity—and we're blessed to be living in America, the land of opportunity—there are no excuses. You simply cannot fail. In launching a business, you can use your own money, or you can borrow and then fail and even if you can't pay your debt, the government allows you to declare Chapter 7 or Chapter 11 bankruptcy. And then you can start again. You cannot fail. Since you have all the opportunities the universe has to offer, you have no excuse. None.

14

Role Models

"Your time is precious, so don't waste it living someone else's life."
STEVE JOBS
innovative entrepreneur, inventor, and home computer pioneer,
cofounder and CEO of Apple, Inc., cofounder of Pixar Animation
Studios, and developer of the iMac, iTunes, iPod, iPhone, and iPad

I would recommend you watch the movie *Jobs*, starring Ashton Kutcher, if you don't have the time to read Jobs's biography. Steve Jobs's story, his relentless vision to start a new computer company, is filled with lessons for the modern entrepreneur. There are lessons in this movie you need to take notice of.

The film is about a college kid who didn't know what he wanted to do with his life. He was bored. With everything. He didn't work well with rules or within societal norms. (Note: I'm not recommending this lifestyle.) He had lots of female liaisons, but committed to none. He used drugs and got high a lot. Reality and the status quo didn't inspire him or fire his imagination. A nine-to-five existence simply didn't appeal to him. He was directionless. Uninspired. Empty.

But one fundamental notion resonated with him, as the movie makes clear: he didn't want to work for anyone.

Sound like you?

One day, lightning strikes. And Steve Jobs is possessed. He's not sure what the inspiration is, or how he's going to pursue it. He *is* sure of one thing: it has to do with technology and computers.

What do Steve Jobs and Apple, the computer company he co-founded, have to do with you and your aspirations to start your own company?

Quite a bit, actually.

It's called a business model. A *business philosophy.*

Steve Jobs wasn't good in school. In fact, he dropped out. School bored him. He wasn't a technological genius. His people skills were horrendous. He was arrogant. He actually abandoned and never visited the child he had with his girlfriend. He bullied people. He fired his friends. He hardly ever complimented others. He was selfish. Some considered him to be insane, or a megalomaniac. When his friends and colleagues pointed out his shortcomings, he simply didn't care what anyone else's assessments were.

But he was relentless.

Nothing and no one would stop him from achieving his objectives.

That last sentence, with some variations, is something repeated at various points in this book. It's worth repeating, because it's important, and it's something that you need to remember at all times.

Now, I'm not saying that you have to duplicate all of Steve Jobs's character traits. I would hope that we can be successful entrepreneurs while still treating other people with kindness and respect.

But it's important to make note of the things that Jobs did right. And remember that before he started, he had *no experience* in business. He was *completely unqualified* to start a company. In fact, he barely had any work experience of any kind.

But his *business model* was sound. He did it right. Perhaps instinctively.

Steve Jobs surrounded himself with the right partners. Like Steve Wozniak, who was the one who actually invented the technology at the core of the Macintosh and with whom Jobs founded Apple Computer.

Jobs didn't create the technology or design the systems that would become Apple. But it was Jobs who created the *industry* that would become Apple. And it was Jobs who came up with the Apple name and brand. He wasn't sure what the technology would be, and didn't know exactly what he was looking for. At one point in the movie, he turns to his team and says, "Give me something new. Give me something everyone can use. Give me something you are passionate about."

Hardly a specific tech direction. And yet that's exactly what his team did. And continues to do.

Jobs had a strong and articulate vision for what he wanted and used that to create the business model for Apple. He minimized financial exposure (in other words, he spent as little money as possible) by working out of his parents' garage. And presto, Apple Computer was born. Apple had no rent to pay, no parking facilities, no insurance. Jobs gave some of his initial team shares in the hypothetical new company, and spent little or no cash.

Steve Jobs then went to a retail outlet—a computer store— and convinced the owner to buy fifty computers that his team would build. He also negotiated to get a higher price per computer and increased the quantity of the order. That initial order started Apple Computer. However, Jobs and Apple wouldn't get paid until they delivered the computers to the store.

Jobs then pursued investors. He was repeatedly and routinely dismissed, but he did not take no for an answer. Take note of that. He continued to look for an investor to provide seed money, until he found one. A former Intel partner was looking for a new start-up. The financial offer from the Intel guy turned into a negotiation and Jobs kept at it, until the Intel guy quadrupled his investment in the new start-up company called Apple. The rest is history.

Jobs's climb up the ladder of success wasn't seamless and it wasn't easy. And it won't be for you, either. Although Jobs had the idea, founded the company, and was the leader of his team, the company that he founded would fire him a few years later.

After being fired by Apple, Jobs then had to go back to square one and put together a new team. Espousing the same business philosophy/model, he soon climbed his way back to the top with NeXT and then Pixar. He subsequently said getting fired was the best thing that had ever happened to him, because he was at his most creative as a beginner.

Meanwhile, Apple had fallen on hard times, and only got back on their feet after acquiring NeXT, which allowed Jobs to return as CEO of the company he founded.

Create your company. Control your company.

Jobs was a leader. And you need to be that in order to be a successful entrepreneur. Jobs was not liked by many people, and it's fair to say he was feared by many people. The people who loved him were loyal to him, and to his "Apple culture." The people who hated him had to sit on the sidelines and watch as he took a start-up from his parents' garage to a worldwide business empire.

Jobs found the seed money to start the company. You will have to do the same to get your enterprise off the ground. Jobs put together a team to implement his vision. And you will have to put a team together to implement yours. Jobs fired anyone who didn't share his vision. You may have to do the same. Jobs fired his friends, without thinking twice about it. Can you? Jobs let no one and nothing stop him from pursuing his vision. Can you?

Say what you will about Steve Jobs, but his last name defined what he did.

He *created* Jobs. He *invented* himself.

Again, I'm not suggesting that you have to be arrogant or selfish or mean-spirited the way Steve Jobs may have been. I'm certainly not saying you should abandon your child and concentrate only on your business.

What I *am* saying is that anything and anyone that takes your time and attention away from your pursuit of success is something that you don't need while you're pursuing success. And that includes family, children, and relationships. At least while you're young and starting out.

Maybe you shouldn't get married or have children for a long time. Maybe you shouldn't waste time hanging out with your friends and doing nothing. Maybe you should be hanging out with people who are brighter and are further up the ladder of success than you are.

It's up to you.

When you're starting out, your every waking moment, including weekends, should be spent on launching your enterprise. Don't let anything or anyone take you away from being committed to YOU.

That's right: don't take breaks.

Don't take vacations.

Pursue something that makes you tenacious and passionate, so you never feel like you need a vacation. Business is life, and your life is your business.

Stay committed to YOU and only YOU. And do that until you've succeeded. You can decide when that is.

Then, once you've succeeded—which may happen in your twenties or may not happen until you're middle-aged—then you can start thinking about a family and love and children and mortgages and car payments and insurance, etc. But there are sacrifices to be made, and some of these sacrifices aren't equal across all lines—gender lines especially. I'll get into this later.

There is an old saying: "If the mountain won't come to Mohammed, then Mohammed must go to the mountain."

In essence, this means that opportunity will not come to you. It won't knock on your door. *You* must create the opportunity (that is, the right thing at the right place at the right time). *You* have to be ready for it, so that if or when it comes, you can take full advantage of it.

It also means that Mommy and Daddy won't be there to wipe your nose, feed you, and create your successful venture, unless your family is already filthy rich and they hand over the family business. And even then, unless you're qualified and ready to take it on, you may well drive the family business into the ground. Someone can open a door for you. You still have to walk through it without tripping and greet what's on the other side, alone.

It means the government won't (and shouldn't) cross all the *t*'s and dot all the *i*'s for you. Living in the Age of Entitlement, we might expect the government to make sure that we're all healthy and happy. But in the real world, entrepreneurs take care of themselves.

Speaking of personal responsibility, you may want to read up on Ayn Rand. She's a punch line, at times, in certain media outlets. But she has a very distinct point of view that we can take to heart, regarding individual responsibility to do well. She opined that if one lives in America, or another free country that gives you both opportunity and free will, that's all you need, and the rest is up to the individual.

She was born a Russian Jewess at the beginning of the twentieth century, and lived through the Cossacks' annihilation of Jews, and barely survived the chaos of Russia's communist revolution. She came to America without being able to speak a word of English and promised herself not to depend on government for anything. Since America gave her the same opportunities as native-born Americans and the freedom to express herself in any way she chose, she promised herself that she would forever be grateful and become self-sufficient.

Rand was opposed to the idea of the welfare state, and that's putting it mildly. She believed that it took away people's incentive to dig themselves out of the slums they were in. She believed that it is the responsibility of individuals to educate themselves and find jobs—and if no jobs are available where they live, then to move to places where they *are* available. In fact, she believed it was one's responsibility to oneself to do so. This principle is known in the business world as having "an inferred fiduciary duty to yourself"—you've heard this phrase before in this book, and you'll hear it again.

Ayn Rand is controversial, and whether or not you agree with her philosophies, I think it's safe to say that the less you depend on government and the more self-sufficient you are, the better off you'll be.

THE ART OF MORE: PRINCIPLE #3

LEARN FROM THE MASTERS

I am an avid reader. I devour information and love history. And, interestingly enough, history books are filled with information that may give you greater insight into how capitalism works. Yes, I've read *Civilization, An Empire of Their Own*, and *Money*. But on their own, they aren't the kinds of books people tend to think of when they are trying to find the "Secrets of Success."

As I learned how the Gutenberg Bible opened up the floodgates of literacy to the great unwashed masses, and especially when I entered my first public library, I became aware that for the first time since the dawn of man, the masses have gotten access to the same information that the rich have. For free.

And now with the Internet, all of human knowledge is also available to us instantaneously wherever we are.

I suppose I could point you in the direction of a few entrepreneurs who have climbed the ladder of success, or other insightful books on the nature of entrepreneurship. But that's too simple. And it would do you a disservice. Because there is no shortcut. All the information you need to enhance your powers of entrepreneurship does not live in one place. Not in one book—not even this one. And not in any one person. No matter how successful they are. And that includes me.

My journey is mine alone. I figured out how to get through my own maze. It may not apply to the journey you will have to make on your own in order to succeed. But it doesn't mean you can't learn something from the success of others.

Who are your role models? Your idols? What can you learn from them? Follow their every move in the news. Watch their decisions and how they conduct themselves. Read their books, learn from their experience, think about how to apply it to your life and goals.

Pick up the *Wall Street Journal* every day and read it. Read about the lives and careers of people such as Bill Gates, Mark Zuckerberg, Warren Buffett, and others, to see what you can learn. Whatever you do, just read.

15

Vacations, Holidays, and Other Wastes of Time

"If you live for weekends—or vacations—your shit is broken."
GARY VAYNERCHUK
Russian-born branding, social media, and retail entrepreneur

Capitalism has made it possible for all of us to enjoy the privileges that were previously reserved for the rich. We have equal access to all the information mankind has amassed in its entire existence. And because of the Industrial Revolution and other wonderful advancements, we now have lots of spare time that would otherwise be filled with menial tasks. Technology, if used properly, can free your day up significantly.

If we are fortunate enough to have a job, we typically work five days a week, and have two days off on the weekend. Sometimes we even get three-day weekends. Most of us with jobs get two weeks off per year in paid vacation days. We also have all sorts of paid holidays off. We get paid sick days. And women get paid maternity leave.

If you add it all up, most of us spend relatively little time working, or focusing on our careers at all. We may even have more time off than actual workdays.

In previous centuries, workdays often lasted ten or twelve

hours, and there were often six or seven such days in a workweek. Wages were a few dollars a week. Vacations were only for the rich.

So here you are, with lots of free time on your hands. And you've certainly gotten used to it. And perhaps expect it.

When you were growing up, your parents may have given you a very comfortable life. So did the school system. You probably went to school from nine in the morning until three in the afternoon. Homework aside, the rest of the day was yours to use as you pleased. You had weekends to yourself. You had holidays to yourself. If you got sick, you could stay home and still get fed.

None of this prepared you for what life is really like.

Right after you graduate from school, you may come to the stark realization that you don't have the slightest idea of how or where to get a job. You probably have no idea how you are going to make a living, much less make your fortune. For one thing, you don't know how capitalism works. You may not know much about economics, but you will certainly still need to understand the basics of a business model if you are going to become a successful entrepreneur.

That means that you will have to think for yourself, and that you will have to educate yourself. And that all of it will be YOUR responsibility.

So I'm going to be your drill sergeant. Let's take a look at the military model for a moment.

Let's say you're eighteen or older and you volunteer to join the military. In boot camp, you will meet your drill sergeant. The person who will put you through hell. The person who will make you do twenty-six-mile hikes. The person who will wake you up at 5 a.m. and make sure that you have no time off.

You are not going to like your drill sergeant. But he's also the person who will make sure that you are ready for battle, and the lessons you learn from him may end up saving your life on the battlefield.

So the guy you hate the most is actually your best friend. Because you *need* a taskmaster. Because without him, you won't force yourself to do it. He has to force you to *be all that you can be.*

You're going to learn responsibility, learn the nature of working with others in a group, and when you're done, you'll be in the best shape of your life. All the things you will need to function in the real world.

As a child, you may have gotten a weekly allowance, or "spending money," but in the real, adult world, you don't get an allowance. You don't get money for doing nothing. In life, if you don't work, you don't make money.

Get used to it.

DON'T TAKE VACATIONS.

There's no reason for you to take a vacation if you're a young person. You can define what young means for yourself. Start at eighteen years of age and go until your thirties.

I have never taken a vacation. I consider work a privilege, not a birthright or means to an end. You actually don't have a God-given right to have a job or to work. If you can earn a dollar, then thank America and its people for giving you the opportunity to work for it.

There are many countries in the world where you would have *no opportunity*, regardless of your work ethic.

In America, where there is all the opportunity you could ever imagine, there are no excuses for goofing off.

This goes for everyone.

Let's say you're one of the lucky ones. You have a job. And you have your entrepreneurial aspirations. Keep your day job.

Pay your bills. Spend the rest of your free time working on your career. Your dream job. Your passionate entrepreneurial venture.

Let's take a look at your spare time, outside of the job that currently pays your bills.

Out of each working week, you get two days off. Multiply that by 52 weeks, and you've got 104 days per year in which you're not working to build your career. Take another two weeks off for vacation, that's another 14 days of doing nothing. You also take off holidays, religious and otherwise.

To me, all of that spells "loser."

You can and should use *all* of the time you have to further yourself. To educate yourself. To dream big. And *do* big.

Don't quit your day job, and do work on your time off.

Do something every day to advance your career.

Ladies, you'll still have evenings free to put on your little black dress and go to the clubs. Guys, you can still go out to a ball game, but don't waste the entire day doing *nothing*. But even these things can be business—networking is business. Bouncing your ideas off of people is business. Gathering contacts is business.

If you're at home on a day off, don't just spend the day in front of your TV like a lump of clay.

Work. Plan. Network.

Get rid of the friends who want you to spend your whole day doing nothing with them. They're not your friends. They're your enemies. Your friends should be cheerleaders for your entrepreneurial interests. Your friends should not suck up all of your valuable time. Like vampires, those friends will leave you lifeless.

The harder you work, the luckier you get.

Work overtime—for yourself.

Entrepreneurs set their own hours and work year-round. Even after they've achieved their goals and even after they're filthy rich.

THE ART OF MORE: PRINCIPLE #4

ALWAYS BE GROWING

To me, a successful life at its most basic is about the pursuit of MORE. That means really going after MORE of the things that lead you to happiness, success, and yes, money. But it doesn't mean keep doing the same thing over and over again to the point of burnout or gluttony. It's about seeking out all the opportunities available to you, considering all your options with care, and executing them effectively with an eye toward bettering yourself in the process. Don't "build a brand" if you're not completely aware of the foundation first.

16

Priorities/Practice
What You Preach

**"Far and away the best prize that life offers is the
chance to work hard at work worth doing."**
THEODORE ROOSEVELT
military officer, historian, adventurer, conservationist,
and twenty-sixth president of the United States

I usually don't care to pry into people's personal lives, even when
I'm giving them advice on life and business.

However, there are certain personal life choices that, generally
speaking, just don't help you.

Reckless spending, for example, doesn't help anyone. Not even
millionaires.

Live well below your means.

I still do.

To get even more personal—try to stay "straight," that is, no
drugs, no booze. You will not win if you don't stay straight. Really.
There's nothing in drugs or booze that will make your schmeckle
bigger, make you smarter, or make you run faster. Also, it costs a
fortune to feed your hunger. And you may get fired when they find
out you're a loser. And you may wind up in jail. And you'll lose
your money. Your date will not be impressed by you throwing up

on her brand-new shoes, as you spout poetic babblings that are meaningful only to you.

If you drink enough, your God-given member won't even work, and the next day you'll feel as if a truck had run you over. You may not even remember what you did, where you were, or who you were there with. Bottom line: if you get hooked on drugs or booze, you're fucked.

I've never knowingly been high or drunk, except in a dentist's chair. I've used that time for other things.

Also, don't smoke. You'll stink like an ashtray, and you'll be playing Russian roulette with cancer. If you lose, you'll die a slow, miserable death.

All of that, because you want to look "cool." It's a waste of your time.

Of course, on the side of the cigarette pack, it says something like "Hey, moron, this stuff might give you cancer or some other disease." In Canada, cigarette packages actually have *pictures* of what cancer does to smokers.

In most public spaces in the United States, smoking is no longer permitted. So if you're a smoker, you end up looking like an addict, sucking on your cancer sticks outside your place of work, or outside of bars, clubs, and restaurants.

There was actually once a brand of cigarettes called Death cigarettes. Not surprising, it was successful.

If you choose to become a smoker, you are an idiot, and you may lack the discipline and intelligence to be a successful entrepreneur. On the other hand, if you have the strength of character to recognize your mistake and kick the habit, then you may have what it takes.

In addition to personal health, the health of your business plan is paramount. A healthy business plan, and a healthy life plan, is one in which you always have a backup plan—in other words, a way to keep paying your bills.

Let's say you're a garage mechanic, and you have big dreams about opening up your own chain of branded garages around the country. Terrific.

While you're working at the garage to pay your bills, what's your backup plan if the garage goes out of business or you lose your job?

Have something else that you can do to pay the bills. Immediately.

Keep your day job and pay your bills, while you're making plans to turn your big dreams into reality.

Should you go to college? The truth is, it really depends on what your career aspirations are.

If you want to become a doctor or lawyer or other high-end professional, then you'll need to attend an institution of higher learning. In fact, you might have to attend medical or law school for as many as twelve years to earn your degree or degrees.

On the other hand, if you're an entrepreneur and aren't sure exactly what you want to do but have really big ideas, I would urge you to dive into the deep end of the pool, right out of high school. Sink or swim. You will learn a lot.

While you're getting your entrepreneurial dreams off the ground, you'll need to limit your financial exposure. In other words, avoid unnecessary spending and save your money.

I will keep making this point in the book.

You need to eat, but you don't really need to eat filet mignon every night or buy bottles of champagne at a thousand dollars a pop. You need clothing that will make you look respectable, but you don't really need a ton of fancy clothes you'll never wear, and will just hang there in your closet.

Do not buy a home. Not when you're starting out.

Live at your parents' home if you have to, and until you can afford to move to a city (I'll get to that shortly). Living at home will always be cheaper, and you'll get home-cooked meals, too. But don't be a mooch. Pitch in with household costs. Buy groceries. But limit your financial exposure. Translation: save on the rent while you invest in your future. I know, it's not "cool" living at home. Try paying your rent with cool.

If you meet a girl you like a lot and you need some private time, rent a hotel room for a night. Make it romantic. Fill the room with music. Splurge on chocolates and roses. When you're done, dump the hotel room, and continue not having to pay rent or a mortgage.

Save the money.

Don't buy a house until later in life. I didn't. The first home I bought was a penthouse on Fifth Avenue in New York, overlooking Central Park. I was thirty-eight years old and I had already made headway toward a fortune—I wasn't about to buy a house if I wasn't already on my way. Until that time, I rented. My monthly rent for a good part of the seventies (until 1979?) was $200.

Renting means that you can pick up and go, without great financial risk. And if you can't afford the rent, or you lose your job, you can move to a cheaper apartment, until you get back on your feet and go back to building your fortune.

Don't buy a home until you have amassed four times the value of the home in your net worth. If you're worth $1 million after tax, go ahead and buy a $250,000 home. And try to minimize the length of your home mortgage. You will also be able to deduct certain monthly mortgage fees, and front-load the "decrease in value" of the home and other legal issues. (For what this all means, I urge you to get legal professional counsel—there's legalese that you have to be ready to dance with, unfortunately. But again, it is up to you to educate yourself. It is not up to anyone else to make it easier.)

Don't buy a car. Certainly not a new one. You may not even need a car. Take public transportation if you can. If you must, buy a secondhand car. But pay cash, don't take out a loan. Buy a rent-a-wreck type car for $1,000–3,000. If you have the cash, pay cash. If you don't have cash, don't buy it.

Buying a new car, even a cheaper model, when you're in your early twenties and don't have a good-paying job or career, doesn't make sense. Even if the car costs $20,000, by the time you're done paying off your car loan several years later, it will end up really costing you $50,000 or more. And that's after-tax money. Which means you'll have to earn even more. And then there's insurance. And repairs. And what if your car gets stolen?

Save the money.

You want to take out a girl and impress her? Rent a nice car. Spending a few hundred bucks is preferable to sticking yourself with a debt of tens of thousands of dollars.

If you really want to splurge, rent a limo for a night. It'll cost a few hundred dollars. You can afford it. And a limo will impress her a lot more than your new $20,000 car. You won't have to find a place to park, and you'll have a chauffeur. And it'll pick you up and drop you off. And when the date is over, the costs of car loans, maintenance, and insurance aren't your problem.

I didn't have a real girlfriend until I was twenty-nine years old, although I had had lots of "girl friends." I also didn't have many of the costs that go along with having a girlfriend. No Christmas gifts. No travel expenses. No nothin'.

I lived at my mother's house until I was twenty-four years old. I contributed to the rent and household expenses, but I had very little financial exposure.

If you don't have the disposable cash, don't buy it. You probably don't need it and can do very well without it.

All in all, these are personal choices. I'm not here to tell you
how to live your life—except, in a way, I am. Your life, in many
ways, is your business—and I'm here to tell you how to be successful in business. The above list of small changes in your personal
life will, I guarantee, help you get to where you want to go.

So, you saved some money, lived at home, and didn't splurge
on a new car. You have graduated from Priorities 101. Now what?
If you live outside or far from a large city, it's time to move to
where the big dogs play. The simple fact is that you will substantially increase your chances of climbing the ladder of success in a
big city.

If you don't live in a big city, move to one now.

Period.

There are more job opportunities in a big city than there are in
a small town. A small town can become a ghost town overnight
when the steel mill goes bankrupt, if that town depends on the
mill as its main source of jobs. And the diners and clothing stores
and supermarkets all depend on those workers having the money
to spend on life's necessities. So if the steel mill goes out of business, the rest of the town's pieces fall like dominoes.

Big cities have more people. Millions of them. Therefore, there
is more money. Big cities have more job opportunities. Many
more. Service jobs for the millions of inhabitants. Construction
jobs for the big buildings. It's almost endless.

As an example, in big cities you can open a pushcart hot dog
stand on the street for very little money. You will make a decent
living selling hot dogs to the hungry people passing by during
lunch and on their way home. You won't have to go to school to
sell hot dogs. You won't have to pay for college. You won't have
working staff; it'll be just you, so you won't have to pay anyone

else. You won't have to pay workers overtime or vacation days, and you won't have to deal with unions.

That doesn't mean you'll become filthy rich with a hot dog stand. But in a big city, you can make a living doing it. And a big city has more people, which means more customers for you.

Big cities can almost guarantee that you will at least have a job. Maybe not the job you want, and maybe not the job that will launch your entrepreneurial goals, but at least you will be able to pay the rent. And while you work at this menial job, you will hopefully have the freedom, and the spare time, to devote all your energies to your entrepreneurial goals.

In the near future, small towns may become a thing of the past. Or perhaps small towns will become idyllic vacation spots for the rich, simply because small towns cannot support or guarantee jobs.

And cities, more and more, are growing outward, so much so that they're becoming mega-cities. Los Angeles now almost touches Long Beach, which almost touches San Diego. The populations of these metropolitan areas are in the tens of millions, and therefore the job opportunities are endless. And with a huge population, it's the perfect place to launch your entrepreneurial venture.

Yes, I know Detroit went bankrupt. And while it may be hard to imagine now, New York City was on the brink of bankruptcy in the mid-seventies. But if you read the newspapers, especially the business sections—and you should, even if you don't understand most of it—you may be convinced, as I am, that Detroit is coming back. And New York came back gangbusters in a relatively short period of time. But if a small town becomes insolvent, or bankrupt, everyone moves away and it turns into a ghost town.

We've been taught to think of small towns as being safer—no gangs, drugs, or violence there. And my chances of protecting my family and keeping them safe are much better in small towns, right?

Wrong. *U.S. News & World Report* recently ran a story about a new study by the University of Pennsylvania that debunks the myth that small towns are safer than big cities. It goes on to report that death from injury of all kinds in small towns is more than 20 percent higher than in larger cities.

Hard to believe, but true.

We all hear the same stories. Big cities have higher homicide rates. Well, true and untrue. Here's the real skinny.

Get ready for this one: The study says your overall risk of being killed by a gun is the *same* in small towns and big cities!

And if you're a child or over forty-five years old, and you live in a small town, you actually have a greater risk of dying from a gun-related event than in a big city, the study says.

To be fair, in big cities, if you're African-American or Latino and you are twenty to forty-four years old and especially if you live in a lower economic sector commonly referred to as the "ghetto," gun-related deaths are higher.

It's no secret. In "ghettos" there is rampant drug abuse, and there are violent gangs on the streets. More deaths per capita occur there than anywhere else in a big city. It's not politically correct to point these facts out, because some people might be insulted.

But it's true. And we all know it. Why this condition exists or how it can be cured is a question for another book by another author. I'm just here to point things out to you that are true, so your decision-making process is clear for yourself and your future.

If you *are* injured or shot in a big city and you need emergency care immediately, hospitals are a few minutes away from anywhere you are.

Small-town hospitals, when they even exist, are often not close to everyone. And small-town emergency staff is not (please forgive me) on the same level as those in big-city hospitals. They are also usually understaffed.

When heads of state need hospital care, they go to big-city hospitals because they want the best care. Small towns, unfortunately, do not have the level of emergency medical care that is found in big-city hospitals.

The best doctors and surgeons are also paid more in big cities, and are attracted to big cities because there are more potential patients and more up-to-date medical facilities.

Sorry. That's the truth.

You may be asking—what is all this talk of health and safety doing in a book about successful entrepreneurship?

It's because these are all factors that need to be taken into account. Health and safety are about preserving life, and life is business. Health, crime, and everything about your life contributes to your chances of success. The more road bumps there are on your journey, the harder it is to get to where you want to go. Crime diminishes your chances of success. You might get injured, killed or robbed. Bad health services/poor hospital care diminishes your chances of success.

So, for your health.

Your safety.

Your job opportunities.

Move to a big city.

THE ART OF MORE: PRINCIPLE #5

LOCATION, LOCATION, LOCATION

Technology has afforded us the ability to connect with people and do business from anywhere in the world, via cell phones, Skype, email, and the Internet. But there is no substitute for (actual) face time and (actually) pounding the pavement. Once you've built a successful business you can conduct meetings via satellite from a yacht if that's your wish, although even the most successful moguls are constantly hands-on with their respective businesses.

Until you reach that point I suggest you do everything you can to be as close to a city as feasible, and keep as low an overhead as possible.

17

Single or Married? Career or Family?

"The only place Success comes before Work is in the dictionary."
VIDAL SASSOON
hairstylist, cosmetics magnate, and philanthropist

A s I've advised elsewhere in this book, you should let nothing and no one stand in your way on the road to success.

First become successful. Then worry about everything else.

This is why I need to address the issues of marriage and family with you at length here. I touched on it earlier, but it bears emphasizing.

Career or family? Often, you can't have it both ways.

Pick one. Choose wisely.

If he or she is demanding more of your time, and if that stops you from pursuing the opportunities you desire, you may have a life decision to make. That may mean you saying, "Right now, my career is the most important thing in my life."

Ladies! Don't let men talk down to you. Or demand more of your attention than you're willing to give, if it interferes with your career goals.

I say career first, relationships second.

Notice I said relationships, plural. You're young. You haven't achieved your career goals and haven't made your fortune yet. So, you don't have kids, you're not married, and you didn't buy a home or car. Right? I *knew* you were smart.

The old family idea was hard on the breadwinner. Dad or Mom went to work in the morning, and the kids didn't usually see them until late at night. We survived, but it was hard and because there was a family that required more of our time, there wasn't an opportunity to try anything else, or take risks.

The more family time you spend, the less time you will have to devote to your career, and the less chance you will have of success in business.

On the other hand, the more family time you spend, the happier you will be. Perhaps. But you may not be very happy if your dream goes unfulfilled, or if an important opportunity passes you by because you spent Thanksgiving dishing family secrets at your aunt's house. In fact, your inability to accomplish your dreams can lead to the destruction of your family—people often take their resentment out on their loved ones. If you pick family over your dream, you may end up losing both.

Beyond matters of the heart, marriage costs money. Lots of it. Marriage—and divorce, which often follows—will be the biggest financial exposure you will ever have.

It will also be the biggest financial commitment you will ever make.

I urge extreme caution. For both man and woman.

Tread lightly. Marriage is fraught with failure. The statistics are not in your favor. And if and when divorce happens, the couple that once loved each other and swore that they would stay together till death, through thick and thin, through good times and bad times, are the same couple who will try to hurt each other, and fight over money and even their children when it is time to divorce.

But we're getting ahead of ourselves here. Can you even afford to get married?

I'm going to say it again, in case you're skimming this book.

Forgive me for speaking bluntly, but this needs to be said, because you, man and woman, need to go into marriage with open eyes and full disclosure before the fact.

If you're a man in your twenties or thirties, and you have yet to make your fortune, I would urge you not to get married. Not yet. You will probably not be able to afford much of anything, other than taking care of yourself.

Also, let's be honest here—you're probably not mature enough to get serious about a committed relationship at this point in your life. I know. I'm a man.

Remember, for legal reasons, I have to stress this is just my opinion. You're free to do as you like. I am here just to put the facts as I see them on the table in front of you. What you do with them is up to you.

If you, the man, get married in your twenties or thirties, you will most likely not be able to support your wife and/or kids. And that's just if you *stay* married.

Statistics tell us that in divorce, the man—if he's the primary breadwinner—will often pay as much as 50 percent of everything he's got—gross, pretax—to his former wife. That means that, at the highest tax rate, he will have to earn *twice as much* to make that money back.

Don't get married until you're mature and secure. If you have no money and no career, taking on the responsibility of supporting a spouse—and children and mortgages and car payments and taxes—just doesn't make financial sense. It may make you HAPPY. But you will be happy and BROKE, and eventually likely DIVORCED, and then you'll have to pay even more.

There is a hierarchy of needs—feeding yourself comes before self-actualization, and love.

Whether you stay single or get married, it's important to *have a business plan.*

If you choose to get married, you both need to sign a prenuptial agreement, which outlines how your assets will be divided in the event of a divorce—with each of you receiving advice from your own attorney so it holds up in court. Without a prenup, when the time to divorce comes, lawyers will be whispering in your ear what a bastard or bitch the other was, and then tempers flare and costs go up.

Better wait until you build your fortune, so you can *afford* to get married or divorced.

The only guarantee you have of never getting divorced is never getting married.

Marriage later.

First, a successful career.

Write that down, children.

And now, a lesson from my personal life. Ladies, unless love overwhelms all logic, don't marry your beloved in his twenties or thirties. He will let you down. He's immature. He may look like a man, but—and believe me, I speak from experience here—at that age we're still just horny little boys on the inside. We're not as mature as you are. We don't have the urge to raise children. We just have testosterone. And lots of it.

Ladies, if you must get married, marry a more mature man of means. The advantages are twofold: a comfortable and safe lifestyle financially, which could mean more freedom for you to pursue your own entrepreneurial goals, and a more mature man who *might* be emotionally ready for marriage and settling down. Notice that I said "might." Also, if you divorce a man of means, you won't have to go back out into the workforce—you will be able to take more risks with your entrepreneurial goals. Unlike the old model, the comfort of marrying someone of means is not a way to kick back—it is a way to give your own career a jump-start, if things go wrong.

I repeat: men, especially, don't get married until after you've made significant headway toward your fortune.

My story?

I stayed single most of my life, without a regular girlfriend. I had no expenses for gifts, travel, and the other costs that come with a relationship.

My first real "girlfriend" relationship was with Cher in 1978, when I was almost thirty years old. Cher was and is a great lady. I moved in with Cher to her home in Los Angeles. After a year or so, Cher decided to move to the Malibu Colony, by the beach. At the time, I was busy working on my first solo album. Cher right-fully asked me to share in the overhead, and I gladly did. I still had my penthouse on Fifth Avenue in Manhattan, for which I was paying $800 per month. I also didn't own a car. I had very few financial obligations of any kind. Not to banks. Not to friends. Not to anyone. This, even after KISS was successful. Please take this example to heart—just because you can afford to throw money away, doesn't mean you have to.

Later, I was fortunate to have a relationship with Diana Ross. Diana is not only an iconic figure to fans around the world, but a wonderful mother to her children. Sometimes I would stay with her, and sometimes at my place in New York. We were together for two terrific years. In the same vein as Cher, we did not cover each other's expenses. We were independent, self-sufficient people. And if you can do that, and if something earth-shattering—like love—doesn't overwhelm your business plan, you should be self-sufficient.

On August 25, 1984, at an event called Midsummer Night's

Dream at the Playboy Mansion in Los Angeles, I met, and was immediately smitten with, Shannon Tweed. I'm sure you can imagine what the party was like.

I was awestruck like I had never been by a woman. She was more mature. More grounded. More in tune with what life is really about. And in a short while, Shannon and I began living together. First she moved into my New York place. Then I moved into Shannon's Los Angeles apartment, where she shared the rent with her sister Tracy and Ruben, their roommate.

Even though it felt like Shannon would be "the one," I was cautious. I have always been cautious. Matters of the heart can take over your life.

After we had lived together for almost two years and had a cohabitation agreement, I decided to buy a home.

The first thing I did was sell my New York apartment. The market was good, and I was able to sell it for a large profit.

I had two years of tax-free use of that capital gain, which was the tax law at the time, so I took my time deciding how, when, and where I would make use of that tax advantage.

It became clearer to me every day that I was falling hard for Shannon, so I decided to buy a home in Los Angeles.

In 1985, I looked around and finally found a two-acre property in Beverly Hills, with a ranch home and guest house on it. I paid cash, against the advice of my business managers. I could afford it. It was well below my earnings and living standard, but I didn't like owing money to anyone—even with the advantages of tax deductions on interest and front-loading depreciation. But more on that later.

Shannon and I lived together for twenty-eight years, without ever having been married. I paid all the bills. Shannon raised the kids. I thought that I never wanted to get married. That's what I had convinced myself of as a young man.

It probably had to do with my father's failings as a business-man, as a father, and as a husband. I decided early on that I would succeed where my father failed.

Unfortunately, that also led to the thick armor with which I surrounded myself. That armor prevented me from being kind, loving, and open to being loved. I didn't want to be hurt the way I had been hurt, the way my mother had been hurt.

So I had to take my own personal journey to connect with matters of my heart, while being duly diligent to keep my business model intact.

So now I am happily married to my beloved Shannon Tweed Simmons.

As I write this, Shannon and I have been together for thirty-one years, but we've been married for only two years.

To put it bluntly, she put up with my sorry ass for all those years, and waited for me to gain a semblance of maturity. It took forever. I was arrogant and selfish and self-absorbed. And I'm ashamed at the lack of respect that I showed her, especially be-cause she was the only true love of my life.

I'm now almost sixty-five years old, and I stayed unmarried until the age of sixty-two. "Will you still need me when I'm sixty-four," indeed.

This is all familiar territory, from the chapter about our show. But my point here is this: I found the right partner, who I knew was in this for the right reasons.

The real truth of why I never got married is that I was afraid. I was afraid of commitment. I was afraid of the financial repercussions.

And statistics tell us I was right to be afraid, even if I was also afraid of my own unethical action. They say it's almost always the man who is the cause of the divorce. He either runs out on his family, or he's not committed enough to the marriage to keep it together. I didn't want to get married, I thought, because there was a huge financial minefield I would have to walk through. This would be true—if I hadn't found the right partner, who for years had verified her intentions to me. It took me too long to realize that she was not a risk to my fortune. She made it abundantly clear.

I was well-read enough to be aware of the community property and cohabitation laws in various states, and I knew all about prenups and other legal maneuvers. I was well aware that holy matrimony was potentially the largest financial exposure I would ever have.

If I got married without a prenup I would be liable for half of everything I had—that's pretax, gross.

Unromantic, I know, but I was afraid.

I walked into our marriage with open eyes and an open heart.

And I could *afford* to get married. Gladly.

But that didn't stop me from also having a prenuptial agreement. Prenups are not the most romantic notions in our society. But I see them as positive reinforcements of one's duties to the relationship. Better to discuss everything out in the open while you're in love, then if or when the relationship sadly ends. It's called Full Disclosure Before The Fact. I would urge all couples contemplating marriage to draw up a prenup. Even the most loving, trusting, and honest relationships can come to an acrimonious end and it's up to me to limit my financial exposure in this litigious society we all live in.

You must do the same. Find a partner—that word again—who is *trustworthy*. And make sure you can afford to trust them, in all senses of the word.

I couldn't have found a better partner. But I got very, very lucky. Be careful out there.

THE ART OF MORE: PRINCIPLE #6

FIND PARTNERS WHO COMPLEMENT YOU

People who try to do it all themselves are destined for a small, limited venture. No one creates a successful business by themselves. You need guys bringing in new ideas and helping you expand. You can't do it all. You don't know it all, and there are only twenty-four hours in a day.

Of course, be sure to trust the partners you make. But more important, trust your judgment of people. Your gut will get you far in business. Before I go into a partnership with someone, I spend time talking to others who know them. I have a legal team research them. I watch them in action, how they manage their life, how they speak to their employees. In business, this is referred to as *due diligence*.

You must employ due diligence in deciding who you are going to work with, in terms of personality and credibility and reliability, and no matter at what level.

18

Brilliant Stupid Ideas/Designing the Right Business Model for You

"Choose a job you love, and you will never have to work a day in your life."
ANONYMOUS
often mistakenly attributed to Confucius

There are many really stupid ideas that wind up being brilliant, if you can implement them.

If I had told you in the early seventies that I had a plan to sell bottled water to people, even though water is already free and you can get as much of it as you want by simply turning on your faucet, you probably would have laughed.

You probably would have been equally unimpressed if I told you that I wanted to get people to pay good money for Pet Rocks, even though you can walk down any street, bend over and pick up a rock, and start treating it as a pet, without paying a cent.

Yet one of these seemingly stupid ideas made its creator a millionaire, and the other became the foundation of an industry that generates $12 billion annually in the United States alone.

There are a lot of massively successful businesses that started out as stupid ideas.

Amazon started selling books online at a time when not many people were using credit cards on the Web.

Craigslist was free and not well designed.

Twitter did less than Facebook, and limited the letter count.

None of these ideas originally sounded like the model for a successful business. In fact, they sounded as crazy and impractical as, say, starting a rock band that wears more makeup and higher heels than your mother.

Your idea doesn't have to be original. In fact, it often helps if it's not.

But your idea is worthless, unless you figure out how to implement it, how to *make it happen.*

That often means you have to create a prototype (in other words, produce the first one as a sample). It also means you have to find the money to do so. And put together your team. And figure out who to sell your product or venture to.

There are also several questions that you must answer.

Do you manufacture it yourself?

Do you raise all the funds to manufacture it yourself?

Do you launch a local campaign, and once you achieve some success, do you then go to a bigger company and sell all or part of your venture?

YOU figure it out.

YOU have to do the research.

And YOU have to do it all yourself. Just like Bill Gates, Steve Jobs, Sir Richard Branson, and Mark Zuckerberg had to do.

While there's some truth to the old saying that ideas are a dime a dozen, if you can implement your idea, and make it happen, the idea grows arms and legs and becomes *real.*

The implementation is more important than the idea itself.

I'm going to do an experiment for you, as I sit here typing my own manuscript.

I promise you, what I write below is something I will daydream, and come up with, right now—unedited. Here goes:

Here's an idea that just hit me: BABY 101. Hmmm. I don't know what it means exactly, but I like the sound of that. Is the name trademarked? Let me check. No, it's not.

Okay, I just told my lawyer to trademark it.

As stupidly simple as this sounds, this is how things often begin. There's a gut sense of something sounding "established," or "sellable." There's this intangible sense that some people have, that something is "catchy" or can be a "catch-all" name for a variety of ventures. The person who came up with "Amazon," for example, may have been thinking of a river of books, but the title is elastic enough to apply to everything and anything under the sun—everything from A to Z. (Incidentally, this expression is incorporated via an arrow in the logo pointing from the A to the Z. Look it up.)

Once I've secured the trademark, I'll need to show that I've used it in other states, to shore up my trademark in the context of interstate commerce laws. So I'm going to make a BABY 101™ T-shirt myself, and sell it to someone I know in New York for ten dollars. And presto, I'm in business! Maybe I'll make a logo for Baby 101 while I'm at it.

So, what *is* Baby 101™? Well, it can be whatever I say it is.

How about this? It's a TV show for young mothers and their babies.

We all have to take driver's end to learn to drive. Then we take a test, and if we pass it, we get a license to drive.

But there's no school for being a mother. There's no public-school course to teach young men and women about the joys and pitfalls of having babies at too young an age. And when the blessed event happens and she gives birth to a healthy and happy baby, then what?

What does the baby eat? How many times a day? Where do I get formula? Clothes? When does the baby sleep? How long?

Does it need to be quiet? Or should I play music? What kind? If the baby is crying, what does that mean? The baby can't talk, and Mom doesn't understand baby talk.

So the daily Baby 101™ TV show—you'll notice I'm using ™ right next to the title, which means it's trademarked—would be a time for new or expecting moms to learn lessons in parenting. And if I *own* the trademark and I'm one of the executive producers of the show, that opens up a truckload of possibilities for merchandising. Of course, I'll have to find a production partner to actually *make* the show, since I don't want to and don't know how to do that myself.

The way I went about getting production partners was relatively easy. At the end or beginning of most TV shows, the production company has a credit. I wrote that information down, or simply Googled which production company did which show. Then, I called and arranged a meeting with the head of the company. Now, I grant you it won't be that easy for you. Remember, a certain amount of celebrity will get you in through the front door. And in my case, it did and it does. But what happens when you sit down together is another thing. The idea or project either has "legs" or it does not. The production company either sees an opportunity to work with me (you), or it does not. Remember, they can come up with their own ideas. But production companies can't come up with every idea. And some ideas/concepts can actually turn into good businesses. Of course, to the extent you can, you must make sure you have some protection, in case people rip off your idea.Then once I find the right production partner, I could call Target or Wal-Mart or another retailer, and tell them that I have a TV show called BABY 101™. And, perhaps the retailer would like to start a co-venture. The retailer BUYS stuff from manufacturers and then SELLS that stuff to customers. Then why not have the retailer manufacture BABY 101™ themselves, since they already have stores that sell baby-related products? Why not have the TV show serve as an infomercial for a line of products? Baby 101 baby food. Baby 101 diapers. Baby 101 instructional books and videos. You get the idea.

As the trademark holder, if I can get the retailer to go into business with me, then I participate in (in other words, make money from) every single step of the process.

Martha Stewart, whom I've met and have long admired, achieved major success using a similar approach. Stewart knows how to cook. So what? Many people do. But what Martha Stewart did was to create the Martha Stewart *brand*—her name, her likeness, her persona, her aesthetic—and then used TV to launch that brand, and then implemented her business model by teaming up with retailers to sell several lines of Martha Stewart–branded products, from cookbooks to furniture.

Remember, she wasn't born with or given any of this, nor do they teach this in school, and no one was aware of a demand for Martha Stewart–branded products until she created the demand.

She did it herself. So did Rachael Ray.

So if you meet a person who tells you that he or she plans to create an industry around himself or herself, it may sound dumb.

But, if they figure out how to implement their idea, then it's an absolutely brilliant dumb idea.

Implementation is what makes a dumb idea brilliant.

THE ART OF MORE: PRINCIPLE #7

BUILD, LABEL, AND SELL

Hardly anyone who is successful (including myself) was born successful. Presidents of countries, corporate heads, rock stars, they all have one thing in common with you: they were born ordinary! The rest comes down to a few variables and a strong work ethic. Yes, luck sometimes plays some part in it. Yes, where you live might increase your chances of succeeding. Yes, who you associate yourself with impacts things greatly. Ultimately, however, it will come right back down to you. To YOU, and how you come off to people.

Keep in mind that we are currently in the new age of business. The value of your name is dominated by computers and the Internet. In social media statistics, for example, KISS currently has more than 12 million fans on Facebook. However, I strongly advise everyone not to rely solely on computers to get the job done—they are merely tools at your disposal toward achieving your goals. But the bigger picture boils down (again) to you. When you sit down for a job interview, the people sitting across from you will put down your résumé and probably say, "So, tell me about yourself." You are your own best résumé. This is your moment. It's always the vacuum cleaner salesman, not the vacuum cleaner, that will make the sale.

19

The Importance of Being Able to Sell Yourself and Tell Your Story

"This is a fantastic time to be entering the business world, because business is going to change more in the next ten years than it has in the last fifty."

BILL GATES

cofounder and former chairman of Microsoft, investor, inventor, computer programmer, and philanthropist

YOU are the business.

YOU are your own boss.

YOU are the BRAND.

Here's what I mean.

Your reputation will precede you. Your name has to *mean* something. As in, "That guy always shows up on time, and always says what he means and means what he says."

Even before people meet you in social situations or job interviews, they will do due diligence on you. "Due diligence" means they're going to do research on you, to find out what *other people* have to say about you. So by the time you finally meet someone, that person will already have an impression of you that's either positive or negative. You want that first impression to be positive.

That means, if the word on you is great before you meet for

that job interview, you're almost home free. And if you continue to get stellar reports on your performance *after* you get that job, it won't be long before you start climbing that ladder of success. It will certainly happen much faster than if you're a schlump and just sit on your thumb.

Brand is a word used to describe all sorts of things, including products. When you go shopping, you are often predisposed to buy this product, rather than that product, because you recognize the brand name and because you have a good impression of the brand name.

If you look at YOURSELF as the brand, then you will understand an intrinsic truth: People judge. They judge everything. They evaluate everything. They will evaluate YOU. They will evaluate you before they meet you. And when they meet you. And once you're gone. They will always have something to say about you before, during, and after. Because your brand, your reputation, will precede you and will always be with you.

It is like a shadow. Your shadow goes wherever you go. So does your brand. Wherever you stand, your shadow will be cast. It is up to you to create a striking silhouette.

It's your responsibility, then, to build and control your brand. Your name. Your appearance. Your speaking skills. Your people skills. All of that needs to happen before you are even qualified to get that job.

And once you get that job, you must *continue* to build and control your brand. That means that you must continue to protect YOU, since YOU are the brand. YOU are in charge of how you come off to people, and it's your responsibility to change if the impression that you're making on people isn't a good one.

If "YOU" isn't working, then change "YOU." Now.

Some people change their looks every six months. Their hair color. Their mode of dress. Everything. They're comfortable changing the look and continually try to figure out which look works better in the real world. At work, they may dress more conservatively. But in the evening, the jackets and ties come out, the skirts might get shorter and the heels higher. Women, especially in this visual way, are great marketers of themselves.

Many women understand that the world judges you visually, and that if the visuals connect, then other facts matter. They recognize that fact, and make it work for themselves.

They teach themselves how to put on makeup. They teach themselves how to be in fashion. In short, they teach themselves all sorts of skills that will increase their chances of success, based on what society has told them is valuable for a woman. Whether this is a good or bad thing is not the point. The point is that, whatever system you are a part of (be it fair or unfair), there are ways to get ahead in it. In the system of business, the modern woman and the modern man teaches themselves what they will need in order to compete.

You'll be judged by your name, your looks, your accent, your everything.

It's an old thought experiment: Two young men walk into a job interview at a law firm. They have similar résumés, backgrounds, and education. One is dressed just in jeans, the other in a suit. Which one gets the job?

And remember, you're not the only one out there. There are plenty of other ambitious people who want what you want, make a better impression than you make, are smarter than you are, are more qualified than you are, and are willing to work harder than you do.

Life is competition. Like it or not, you will always be in competition with others. Which is why it's important for you to be the caretaker of YOU.

By the way, I keep capitalizing YOU to get your attention. To keep pointing back at YOU. To kick YOU in the butt and make YOU do it now.

As the Nike people say, "Just do it."

In America, we are a multicultural melting pot where there is equal opportunity for all. Well, almost.

Equal *relative* opportunity, for those with the same skills and abilities. But even then, the best of the best will get higher. Life and nature pick the strongest.

"We are all created equal" is simply not true. Never has been and never will be. Some of us are born smarter. Some are born faster, live longer, are stronger, and so on.

Once you recognize and understand that, you'll begin to see that the only way you'll beat the smarter/better-looking/younger/more experienced guy is simply to work harder and longer and never give up.

"Equal opportunity" simply means that there's lots of opportunity in America. It will never be "equal," because the world is populated by human beings, and human beings have their prejudices. All of us. You. Me. Everyone.

The United States of America is the richest country in the history of mankind (although China is soon to be). The United States is also one of the youngest countries. Other countries and cultures have been around for thousands of years. Yet in under two and a half centuries, America has been able to invent flight, develop the assembly line, put a man on the moon, and make all the other endlessly repeated accomplishments you tend to hear from people like me.

Although we have a constitution that says that all people are created equal, that's an ideal, not reality. Worth repeating: some people are born faster, some are smarter, some are shorter, some are fatter, some are thinner. We believe that our rights should supersede our inherent natures, supersede our DNA. Perhaps they should. But in the real world, they don't.

So we all have to *fight* for the rights we are guaranteed under the Constitution: to be treated equally under the law, and not to be profiled or incur prejudice and other notions, like being judged by what we look like and sound like.

All good, except that you're dealing with human beings. And I contend that human beings, either by nature or nurture or culture or religion, are fundamentally judgmental and prejudiced.

First impressions are incredibly important. When you meet a new person, that person's first impression of you will often make or break you. As the old saying goes, you only get one chance to make a first impression. Like it or not, other people will judge you.

Members of just about every group have had to fight to overcome other people's prejudices or preconceptions about them. Whatever their sources, those prejudices are a part of life, and they're not likely to change drastically in our lifetimes. Or perhaps ever.

Therefore, in the areas that you *can* control, you may as well do your best to make things work to your advantage. Let's start with your outer appearance. How you dress. How you speak.

Let's say you're a Hasidic Jew (and I was one) and you want to be a TV newscaster in America. So you arrive with your yarmulke, beard, fur-covered hat, and long black jacket, and you interview for the job. Now let's say the TV station actually takes a chance on you and puts you on the air. How many people do you think would actually watch the evening news if it were hosted by someone who looks like you? You might have substance and important things to say, but viewers will judge you by your appearance, which will be alien to most Americans and thus unwelcome. I contend that the masses *listen with their eyes*, rather than actually listening to what is being said. Which is why there has never been a Hasidic newscaster on American television. And there likely never will be.

Remember, I'm Jewish, so I'm not being anti-Semitic here. I'm just being pragmatic and pointing out that in the world we live in, your outward appearance is important, and that it's particularly important if you plan on being a successful entrepreneur. Trees that don't bend with the wind break in two.

Be flexible.

Get over yourself.

So when you've got that big job interview, or you're ready to meet with that banker or potential investor to launch that great big entrepreneurial venture, leave the yarmulke or dashiki or turban at home. You can proudly express your ethnicity, culture, and religion at home. But in business situations, wear the costume that your colleagues and potential benefactors will like. This means a nice haircut and a suit and tie if you're a man. And if you're a lady, don't show too much skin or wear too much makeup. For better or worse, banks and financial institutions are still a boys' club, and you should promote yourself and your skills, not what you look like. Otherwise, you will not be treated seriously. Again— this is a prescription for success in business, not life. At no point in this book will I contend that I have the authority to decide how much skin women should or shouldn't show, or what they should dress and look like. That is none of my business, if it's not business. But in the business world, there happens to be a dress code for success.

You wouldn't wear loud, bright colors to a funeral, and you wouldn't wear sexy clothes in a church, temple, or mosque. The same rules apply in business. If you own an auto repair shop or a tattoo parlor, or if you're in a rock band, then you can ignore those rules. Otherwise, forget it. Maintain the proper appearance at the proper time, at the proper place, in front of the proper people.

I'm sorry if I'm not being politically correct here, but if you're looking for sugarcoating, go buy another book. I'm here to help you make the Big Money, not to tell you what you want to hear.

A lot of people are afraid of offending you. I'm not. Because I'm *one* of you. Like millions and millions of other Americans, I wasn't born in America. I look like I come from somewhere else. And millions and millions of you do, too.

The difference between myself and a lot of other people is that I decided long ago that I would adapt as best I could, and that I would conform, to the extent that I could, to the inferred rules of culture in these United States of America. Yes, you heard that right—I'm a *conformist.*

There are inferred social rules in every country, but in America, you have the choice to follow them or ignore them. But I contend, if you choose to ignore these rules, a much more difficult path to the Big Money lies ahead of you.

Another thing: *Do not use slang in business situations.* Using words like *dude* and *man* in front of business professionals will make them think that you're an idiot.

Which leads to my next point.

THE ART OF MORE: PRINCIPLE #8

KNOW WHO YOU ARE SELLING TO

Everything costs money, and people need to give you money for the service or product you offer for sale. You have to figure out how to get your stuff into their hands and get their money into your hands, and therein lies the big hurdle. How do you do that for the least amount of money on your part, for the most amount of money on theirs, and how do you get them to understand they can't live without your stuff? You must know your audience, customers, clients, and what they are expecting from you.

20

Speak English

"I went into the business for the money, and the art grew out of it. If people are disillusioned by that remark, I can't help it. It's the truth."
CHARLIE CHAPLIN
actor, film director, author, songwriter, and studio founder

Another important point: *learn to speak English.*

There's nothing wrong with being proud to be Spanish or African-American or Albanian, but that in itself won't help you amass a fortune in America. And bluntly speaking, English language skills can. Anywhere in the world. Speak English in Zimbabwe, and you can get a job. Speak one of the hundreds of Zimbabwe dialects in America, and it won't help you in the least.

And try to speak English without an accent. Please! Again, this book isn't about being politically correct, it's about showing you how to make money. Let's be real. If I can't understand what you're saying to me, or if your accent is too strong, the impression I'll get won't be about the content of the conversation. It will be about your accent.

I'm here to tell you that politically correct notions hardly ever tell the *real* truth, the whole truth, and nothing but the truth. Political correctness is probably well intentioned. And things like "slander" often result in lawsuits.

Whether or not a lawsuit has merit, it still costs a lot of money to defend. So most of our institutions—the media, the education system, politicians, employers, and corporations—are very careful about what they say, how they say it, and who they say it to.

So let me spell it out plainly for you, from one immigrant to all the rest of you immigrants out there: LEARN TO SPEAK ENGLISH. And learn to do it well. And learn to speak it without an accent. Really.

I know you're proud of where you come from. And you're proud of your heritage, your religion, and your customs.

Terrific. You're proud of yours. And I'm proud of mine.

So what?

Unless and until all the different cultures and languages and religions who immigrate to America figure out how to get along with each other in the same country, there will be chaos. The Tower of Babel.

And that means we all have to give in a little, and get off our high horse regarding our languages and our cultures and even our religious beliefs.

Get over yourself.

I do want to put forward this caveat: There are no absolutes. There are and always will be exceptions. You might have a wonderfully thick Indian accent, be a mathematics wiz, and be gloriously successful on Wall Street.

In public schools, your teacher will never tell you that your thick accent or lack of English speaking skills may hinder you on your climb up the ladder of success. If she did, she'd be fired. Even though it's the truth.

Your teacher will never tell you (God forbid) that people in America, right or wrong, simply don't react well to thick accents or lack of English speaking skills.

But it's true. And this may be an unfair reality that you will have to contend with.

And your boss at your job, if you have one, will never tell you to your face that your thick accent may tinge or somehow affect his perception of you. That would not just be politically incorrect, but illegal, as well.

Yet, sometimes, it's the truth.

I don't play by those rules. You don't work for me, and I can state my opinion as I please.

Especially, since I *was* one of you.

In 1958, when my mother and I legally immigrated to America, I couldn't speak a word of English. Neither could my mother. We spoke Hungarian and Hebrew, and my mother knew halting German. I also picked up (and have since forgotten) some Spanish and some Turkish.

My mother couldn't speak English and didn't have an education, so she wound up working in a sweat shop. Six days a week. No holidays. No minimum wage. It was the only job available to her in New York with her skill level.

I wasn't born in America, but as a young boy, I quickly learned that the more foreign I sounded, the less I was accepted into the mainstream.

One of the first things I remember hearing when I was eight and a half years old was "What're you, stupid? Can't you even speak English?" I would never forget that. It was unkind and harsh, yes. But it was an uncensored reflection of how native-born Americans might consider you if you aren't able to communicate in English. The less ability you had to speak English, the more stupid most people thought you sounded.

It was true then, and it's true now. And it will be true tomorrow, as well, to varying degrees. We can strive to change it—to make positive social change is a worthy endeavor. But if you want to be a businessman, you have to contend with the way the world is right now, not the way you would like it to be.

Sorry. That's life. You can't force everybody to think the way you do.

Encouraged by the predominant American culture, I forced myself to learn to speak American English. Either I did that, or I would continue to be made fun of, have fewer friends, play on fewer baseball teams, and be invited to fewer parties. And at that age, those things were important to me.

I learned to speak English without an accent and graduated from college with a bachelor's degree in education. I was immediately able to start teaching sixth grade to native-born Americans. I spoke better English than they did. Then, at age twenty-two, I became the assistant to the director of the Puerto Rican Interagency Council. Those were some of the jobs available to me with my skill level, once I learned to speak well.

Put in the work.

Get the results.

I'm here to increase your chances of success, so I'm not going to sugarcoat any of the obstacles that might hold you back. And your thick accent and/or lack of English speaking skills are not your friends. Try to get rid of them. Now.

"He's well-spoken," they'll privately say to each other.

And lest you think they're picking on you just because you come from someplace else, consider this: that same sentiment is held by Americans about each other. For instance, if your accent is too "southern"-sounding, many Americans might assume you to be, uh, less than sophisticated.

It would be difficult for most Americans to take Professor Billy Bob Fitz seriously, if his first direction in Shakespearian studies at the university was "For tonight's assignment, y'all consider the dilemma Othello had to live with, mmkay?"

I won't apologize for the parody, or my crudeness—this is a crude, unaccommodating world you are going to step into. Grow a thick skin and *adapt*. Be a Darwinian apex predator—whatever your environment, adapt to it, and conquer it. It just so happens that the business world in the United States is an English speaking environment.

It also bears noting that, in the southern United States, TV broadcasters rarely sound southern. They all speak in perfect "mid-Atlantic" American English, even if they were born in the South, love the South, and eat grits. They realize that the sound of their accent does not connect to the rest of the country.

Lest you southerners think I'm singling you out, you're not the only ones.

A heavy New York accent, with its "deze" (these) and "doze" (those), is considered by many to be less than sophisticated. To be blunt—it makes you sound stupid.

I didn't invent the rules.

Unless you're sitting on a large oil deposit in your backyard in Texas, you will note that the large corporate giants and captains of industry, who are worth billions, like Bill Gates and Warren Buffett and Mark Zuckerberg, all speak mid-Atlantic American English.

That's no coincidence.

And lest you think I'm only talking about white people.

President Obama speaks mid-Atlantic.

Oprah Winfrey speaks mid-Atlantic.

Wendy Williams speaks mid-Atlantic.

YOU can learn to speak mid-Atlantic well.

I do.

When in Rome, do as Romans do.

You're in America, and while we may not, on paper, have a national language, it's simply counterproductive not to do what will make you the most money—what will help you thrive. And right now that means learning to speak English.

The better you can communicate in English, the more money you stand to make.

Let's not stop there. Let's go all the way. Buckle up. It's gonna get bumpy.

Speaking with a heavy Yiddish accent that isn't easily understood by the masses will not help you advance. It doesn't matter that you're proud and it's your heritage. No one else cares. Really.

Speaking with a very heavy accent will usually not help you make more money. There are always exceptions, of course, but why take the chance?

A heavy French accent for a maître d' in a French restaurant? Sure. Fine.

A heavy French accent for an American TV newscaster? Not so fine.

And not speaking English at all will buy you an express ticket to the bottom of the barrel.

It's YOUR responsibility to learn to speak English properly.

Nobody will tell you this, because it's supposed to be unkind. It's politically incorrect. It will hurt the feelings of immigrants.

So, I will.

SPEAK ENGLISH!!!

I had to do it.

You can, too.

I wrote some of this book dictating into my iPhone. Siri takes pretty good dictation. Siri and I get along great. She understands every word I say. That's because I speak very good mid-Atlantic American English.

Siri becomes less and less reliable the heavier your accent is. She may have other language settings—but people don't.

Take a hint from Siri.

She knows.

She doesn't care if you're a nice person.

She only cares if she can understand you.

If Siri doesn't understand you, then you're in trouble.

As I've said elsewhere in this book—there are, and will always be, exceptions to every rule. We were at a basketball game at Staples Center in Los Angeles. And on the way out, someone introduced me to former California governor Arnold Schwarzenegger. The first words I spoke to him were in German. I'm fairly fluent in the language and we exchanged banter. He was born in Austria and went into bodybuilding seriously. He soon rose through the ranks. When he arrived in America, with few English language skills, he soon won Mr. Olympia and other bodybuilding titles. Note that he chose a first career that had little to nothing to do with language skills. A smart move. Then he segued into movies, playing the kinds of roles where his physique was the draw. Before too long, he became the world's top box-office draw. He then turned his attention to politics and easily won the election to become the governor of what was then the sixth-largest economy on earth: California.

Whatever hurdles you may think are in front of you as a native-born American, imagine coming from another country and culture, with no English speaking skills. And with an unwieldy name that's difficult to spell and pronounce.

Still, the same strong backbone that enabled him to come to America and rise to the top of the bodybuilding world, and then the film world and finally in politics, says something about who the person is.

Remember, every step of the way, people made fun of how he

pronounced English words, and how he spelled his name. None of it mattered to him. Nothing would keep him from succeeding.

Take note—his accent was something he had to overcome. It isn't impossible. But you will have to work for it.

Champions are not born. They work for it.

THE ART OF MORE: PRINCIPLE #9

SPEAK THE LANGUAGE OF MONEY

You don't need an MBA to make it in business—but there are some basic facts about money everyone should know. The entire economy is based upon the notion that money must exchange hands for it to continue to live. The more you understand that, the more you will find access to others people's money in pursuing your endeavors.

21

Women Entrepreneurs

This chapter is specifically designed for you, women entrepreneurs.

I won't get into how humiliating and arduous a climb you've had to make in order to gain respect and win control of your own lives in this country, and others. I also understand that your struggle is not over yet. In many African, Asian, and Middle Eastern countries, women are still being treated like property or worse. And we've still got a ways to go in the United States, though the misogyny we experience here is slightly less obvious, and slightly more insidious.

But here in Western society, and particularly in America, women have the opportunity, perhaps more than at any time in history and perhaps more than anywhere else on earth. So there's really no excuse for not becoming an entrepreneur.

If you've got the guts.

For role models, men can look up to many successful male

entrepreneurs who started with nothing and created business empires for themselves. The list is long. Bill Gates/Microsoft. Mark Zuckerberg/Facebook. Steve Jobs/Apple. Sir Richard Branson/Virgin. All of these men started with no funds, had no prior experience, and forged ahead nonetheless.

Women should take note that there are role models for them to look up to as well.

The following women play to win in a man's world. Because it *is* a man's world, unfortunately. And men will not soften the rules to suit you, just as they won't soften the rules to suit other men who don't make the grade.

Please note, as well, that none of these women I'm about to name married into their position, or were born with a crown on their heads. They had to fight hard to get where they are. Perhaps harder than their male counterparts. And they deserve the respect and admiration of all of us for being able to overcome any obstacles that society and culture put in front of them.

They won, regardless.

And, you can, too.

German chancellor Angela Merkel oversees Europe's most thriving economy. The German gross domestic product (GDP) is almost $12 trillion. Merkel became chancellor the old-fashioned way. She worked for it. She didn't marry into it. She didn't inherit it. She clawed her way to the top, went toe to toe with men, and won.

Marillyn Hewson is the CEO of Lockheed Martin, the global aerospace, defense, security, and tech company. Hardly a position one would associate with a woman. But there she is atop an entity populated with mostly men.

Ellen Sirleaf Johnson is the head of state of Liberia. She is one of two recent female heads of state in all of Africa. The other was

Joyce Banda of Malawi. Both ladies routinely met to improve the lives of women living in Africa.

Ginni Rometty is the CEO of IBM. Computers. IBM is led by a woman—the old stereotype of technology not being "feminine" is crumbling.

Meg Whitman is CEO of Hewlett-Packard. Before that, she ran for governor of California and lost by a small margin. She was also president and CEO of eBay.

Marissa Mayer heads Yahoo. When she came on as CEO, the company was in tatters. Under her leadership, Yahoo has made a complete turnaround.

It bears noting that during the five years that Mayer worked at Google, she did 250 all-nighters. Think about that: 250 nights with no sleep to get the job done.

So why not you? Do you have that kind of dedication to succeeding? Can you do it?

It was clear, even in the beginning, that Marissa Mayer was willing to outwork her coworkers.

Although Mayer is married, when she comes home from work, she doesn't stop working. She will work late into the evening, even though she is with her husband. She doesn't stop working just because she's at home.

And that's the sign of a champion.

Breathe it. Feel it. Dream it. Be it. All the time.

YOU are the engine that makes it all happen.

You are a car battery: you must recharge by turning on and running, every day.

Ladies, first and foremost: you're on your own. No more rules neatly laid out for you to follow. You have to make up YOUR OWN rules.

And quite honestly, that's tougher for women, because you

don't *have* to do this for yourself. As a woman, there is a social contract, and a social stereotype, that teaches you from an early age that you always have a security blanket, called a man. You have the option of getting married, having children, and spending all your time caring for the home, while he is working and trying to pay for it all. This persistent stereotype is still here, and though it's not enforced as rigorously as it was in the fifties, it is still prevalent. Some people, sometimes, will wonder why you're "bothering" to work so hard, instead of just settling down.

And you can certainly do that. It's your life.

But if you decide to be a homemaker or a stay-at-home mom, you may as well leave your entrepreneurial aspirations at the door of the home that you didn't get to buy.

The biological clock that keeps tugging at women to have children before their middle years, and the male culture that keeps shoving this message down their throats, is probably the biggest obstacle to them devoting all of their waking moments to their careers. If you're a woman, your early twenties to your forties is the most important time to work at your aspirations. Without any diversions.

So your biggest decision to make is this: do you want to devote all of your energies in your twenties, thirties, and forties to your career goals, or do you want to conform to a biological imperative, a traditional social stereotype, and be a stay-at-home wife and mother? Again—there's nothing wrong with this. At all. But at this point in history, perhaps for the first time, you truly don't have to. The vistas of possibility are becoming wider, and grander, all the time, because of trailblazing women like the ones mentioned above.

Sometimes you do have to make that hard, fork-in-the-road choice. Sometimes there simply isn't enough time to be a mother and wife and also have career aspirations. I certainly recognize that millions of strong women are single mothers. And I recognize that those women raise their own children, as well as going out and working for a living. But a lot of them are just working to pay the bills.

If you want to increase your chances of becoming a successful entrepreneur, if you want to climb the ladder of success, you *cannot* let anyone or anything get in your way. That includes your biological urges, and the social stigmas that enforce them.

Not until you've hit the big time!

You can't pay enough attention to matters at home and at your career at the same time. There just aren't enough hours in the day.

Statistics tell us that if you decide to have offspring, it's best to have *one*. Just one. At least when you're in your twenties. Because one may be manageable in terms of time, cost, love, and effort. To use a corny analogy, if you're a "plate spinner"—you know, those people who keep multiple plates spinning on top of a stick—it's best to have only one plate to spin, instead of ten. If you have more than one plate spinning at the same time, you will constantly be running back and forth trying to keep every plate spinning. It is inevitable that no matter how hard you work, the longer you spin, the greater are the chances of dropping them all.

What I am about to say is politically incorrect, and may hurt the feelings of people of faith or offend your racial or cultural considerations. Too bad. Here goes.

Don't have a big family—especially if you can't afford to have one.

Statistics also tell us that lower-income Hispanic, Italian, white, and African-American families tend to have kids at an early age, sometimes with a parent in their teens. This is lunacy, and it must stop.

For your children's sake.

And for yours.

If you must have children at a young age, have one. Maybe two. That's it.

Sorry, the rich are different. They can have as many kids as they like, *because they're rich*. They can afford the extra cost of feeding, clothing, educating, and nurturing multiple people. A child is like anything else—you have to determine if you can afford to have one. If you can't, then don't have one.

There's more.

According to a U.S. Department of Agriculture study, raising just one child through its eighteenth year will cost you anywhere from $241,080 to $500,000. That's after-tax money, which means that, depending on your tax bracket, you can add between 30 and 50 percent to that figure, meaning that, at the highest tax rate, you will have to earn anywhere from $500,000 to $1,000,000 to raise one child until the age of eighteen!

Now, multiply that by the number of children people have, and you have a financial model that simply cannot bear a quality of life your child needs.

Again. STOP HAVING SO MANY CHILDREN.

NOW.

Generally speaking, women often have two choices in life, as a matter of sheer economic pragmatism: devote all of your time to your career, or have a family and children. There are scores of books debating whether it is feasible to do both, but personally, whether it is or not, I don't think it's worth the risk, most of the time. Better to play to win, and have a family after you've already accomplished something.

Men don't have that option and don't have that choice. They *have* to go to work. They can't give birth and traditionally (as part of a social stigma that enforces a stereotype) don't have the inclination to stay at home and raise the kids. This is changing all the time. Soon this may be irrelevant. However, I'm talking about the here and now—and these old fifties models still seem to apply to millions of people.

That goes all the way back to *Australopithecus africanus,* one of our early ancestors, who lived on the plains of Africa a few million years ago. He hunted and gathered. The female wasn't as strong or as fast, and generally had to depend on the kill that he brought back. Things have certainly changed since then. But these traditional roles still seem to carry weight in our cultural memory. The bigger the piece of meat he brings back, the more attractive he is to the females (please address your hate mail to my post office box).

So, yes, you can choose to be a housewife, and forsake your career aspirations. But if you do, YOU will be the last in line. Your children will come before you. Your husband is also more important. When everyone else is happy, *then* you get to be happy.

Wanna be the most important one?

Then you have to make some real choices in your life.

You often can't have it both ways (more on that later).

Pick one: CAREER or FAMILY.

It can't be fifty-fifty.

It all comes back to YOU.

Men who thrive in the workplace, they live it. They breathe it. They eat it. In sports, in military combat, in the workforce, there are men who compete and thrive. They *want* to win.

Every day.

And, there are women who do these things. There are women who *want* to win.

I hope you are one of them.

There are some huge hurdles that you'll need to overcome. Culture, misogyny—hell, guys like me. Old-world guys who enforce misogynistic stereotypes almost unconsciously. You'll need to beat us at our own game. But, mostly, you need to overcome YOURSELF.

There are statistics in business journals, in medical journals, in social scientific journals that tell us that the biggest challenge to becoming a successful lady entrepreneur is the lady herself, YOU.

And of course, men still won't accept you as the powerful woman you will become. Men still have preconceived notions about you. Men still look at you physically, and if you're very attractive, they find it hard to look past all that.

Too bad.

I didn't invent any of this.

Fight it.

Or ignore it.

But make it work for you.

So let's take a look at what the *facts* are about women in the workforce.

And let's then take a look at why none of that should matter to you on your way to the top.

First, some bad news. Studies tell us that many women are dropping out of the workforce by the end of their twenties.

Coincidentally, these years tend to be important ones for family and child-bearing. And because you're reading this book, this will not stop you, right?

Now, some good news: at entry-level positions in corporations, women account for about half of the jobs.

Bad news: over time, men are twice as likely as women to advance up the corporate ladder. Why is this? Is it a result of a zero-sum situation: "Do I want to have someone else raise my children while I put my full focus on my career?" Is that a result of nature or nurture? Who cares? It simply is. And that means that you'll have to work harder than he will.

More bad news: we are told only 3 percent of technology

companies are started by women. That means that 97 percent of technology companies are started by men.

Research also tells us that 98 percent of all companies owned by women never make more than $1 million a year.

Why? If you're a social activist trying to effect positive change in the world, this question bears weight. If you're an entrepreneur, it doesn't matter why—this is simply the monster you have to defeat, regardless of the reason it was born.

Also, consider this:

Men are the predominant readership of news and financial journals like *Bloomberg Businessweek* and the *Economist.* Female readership of these publications is only 27 percent.

Men also are the predominant readers of sports publications, which I contend reinforce issues of competition and teamwork.

Women account for about 75 percent of the viewing audience of TV shows like *Ellen* and *The View.* I contend that none of these female-skewed shows help women to advance in business.

Make of this what you will.

Perhaps as a woman who wants to immerse herself in the business world, you may consider turning your TV set to Bloomberg and listening to the captains of industry talk instead. Read *Entrepreneur* and *Forbes* and other business journals. Visit websites devoted to female entrepreneurship. Check out entrepreneur.com and go from there. Educate yourself. Hang with friends who are already in the fields in which you want to succeed. Unfortunately, that usually means: hang out with men. It's up to you to change this over time.

Steve Harvey is right: Act like a woman. *Think* like a man. Specifically, think like the men who are accomplishing what you want to accomplish. That way, once you start doing it, it won't be the province of men anymore.

I'll never forget the film *A League of Their Own.* It's about a female baseball team during World War II. Tom Hanks is their coach. One of the players on the team starts crying when she strikes out.

Hanks yells at her: "There's no crying in baseball."

As a woman, do you want to be respected in the workforce?

Want to be taken seriously?

Want to be treated as an equal among men?

Then don't ask for a handicap, and don't accept one. Don't accept coddling; don't succumb to female stereotypes.

The men around you may come over and try to console you as you're sniffling, and ask you what's wrong, but secretly they really don't want to do that, and quite frankly, they don't care. They're probably sharks gunning for the job you want.

Just like in the suppressed fifties, men at work can't cry.

And neither can you.

Not in the business world.

Want to cry? Go outside.

"There's no crying at work."

And *don't gossip.* Whatever the stereotype is—and yes, I'm aware these are stereotypes—don't embody them. Don't embrace them. Reject them with all your might. Convince old-fashioned guys like me that we really were wrong when we labeled you with this stuff.

Don't gossip about work or at work.

Wanna gossip? Go to the newsstand, buy your favorite gossip magazine, and gossip about Jennifer Aniston. Not about your co-workers or your job.

You already have enough working against you in this male chauvinistic world, so you don't need to add fuel to the fire by gossiping and giving anyone else a reason to dismissively point out, "Yeah, well—she's a girl."

Don't do that.

Become enormously successful, and then make all those simplistic, Cro-Magnon cavemen work for YOU.

Living well is the best revenge.

You want that, right?

And dress for success.

Go into business meetings and act like the men whose jobs you want.

Don't dress or act too sexy. Men don't understand nuance and subtlety. Really. The men will pay attention to your sexiness, not your brain or what you have to say. And that's not what you want.

This is not to decide what you should and shouldn't look like—if I see a man at the office wearing bicycle shorts, you better believe I'm going to tell him how to dress, too. He should be wearing the uniform of the position he wants. And so should you.

This is not a book about being happy in life, or about personal liberty—this is a book about being successful in BUSINESS. Specifically. You should be able to dress however you want, whenever you want, for whatever reason you want, in life. In the office, dress for the job you want, and dress to deliver a message: You are not here to be a sexual object, or to express yourself. You are here for a job, and you are here to defeat your competitors. Dress for that.

I'm being blunt. Because other books won't.

Come into that meeting dressed like your boss.

That's right, *dress like your boss.*

Women like Hillary Clinton understood that long ago. She has been wearing business suits for a long time. And she may have a chance of becoming president of the United States, if she decides to run. I'm not saying I would or wouldn't vote for her. I'm simply saying she understands she must play by MALE RULES, until she can make them HER RULES. Beat us at our own game. Take the misogyny of our culture, make it yours, and after you've seized power, turn it against us. You can rewrite traditional gender stereotypes after you've conquered the system. Not before.

Women are nearly absent in Silicon Valley, and in mathematics, and the sciences, and in architecture and construction.

That's not bad news.

That's good news.

That means by entering into these areas, as a woman, you have nowhere to go but up.

Yes, you will find sexism, prejudice, and chauvinistic male attitudes. Many men will still not take you seriously. They've been in these workplaces forever. Women haven't, either because society didn't allow them or because they were not attracted to these areas. In either case, the result is the same: women have been largely absent from these fields.

As a woman, you need to wrap your head around career opportunities that you wouldn't normally consider.

It also bears noting that it's never too late to start on your journey to become a successful entrepreneur. Even after your children have grown up, and they're off on their own path. If your children have left the nest, you will have lots of time to devote to YOU. And that's exactly what you'll need. Time. Lots of it.

For African-American and Hispanic women in low-income brackets, believe it or not, the news is actually good. Despite being in lower-income areas, despite not having access to funding (banks will often not take the risk of lending to lower-end economic groups), despite not being ingrained in the social circles of the white-male-dominated business world, African-American and Hispanic women are three to four times more likely to start a business for themselves than their white counterparts.

The above is worthy of high praise, because the pressures of being an African-American or Hispanic woman are compounded by the fact that 70 to 80 percent of black and Hispanic households don't have a father at home. Let's not romanticize any of this. It's simply fact. African-American and Hispanic women need to work harder than their white female counterparts—to defeat the facts, and to defeat the stereotypes that enforce the facts.

Additionally, African-American women marry at a rate of about 40 percent—much lower than their white counterparts. Even if married, divorce rates are very high.

And I'm not even broaching the *cost* of having a family and children. With a family, you're spending for three or four people, not just for yourself.

All of which places enormous burdens on the minority female who wants to be a lady entrepreneur. Family and children are supposed to come first, but—and it's difficult to say this—a lot of the time, it can't!

I'll say it again: I raise my glass in toasting the extraordinary obstacles that African-American and Hispanic women are overcoming to go after their goals. With or without men.

You, the female entrepreneur, must mingle and be socially active in men's groups, business conventions, and often (unfortunately) in predominantly white male business groups. That's where the money and power are.

Go down to Wall Street and walk through the corridors of power. You will see an overwhelming white face.

Network.

Schmooze.

Put YOUR FACE up there.

Anywhere and everywhere there is a chance to mingle with other businesspeople. Daytime. Nighttime. Weekends.

There's some more good news and some more bad news.

First, we are told that women consume more than men do. I mean much more.

And that means companies and advertisers and broadcasters and print media and Internet companies are constantly trying to figure out how to sell stuff to women.

That is good news for women, if they can take advantage of this power.

Now the bad news.

The manufacturing world, the industrial world, and the tech world are run mostly by men, with few exceptions. Even in stereotypically traditional roles—women cook, but the big chefs are men. Women care about fashion, but the big fashion houses are predominantly run by men. Men also run big hair salons—for women!

For a potential lady entrepreneur, this is a huge opportunity. The bad news is good news for you. There is nowhere to go but up.

You should be aware that most of the stuff that's sold online is bought by women. And that's good for you, lady entrepreneurs, because you know what women want. You *are* women. In social circles, and with your gut, you can tap into a marketplace that men struggle to understand, and yet somehow command. There is a feminist revolution waiting to be had here.

Companies and advertisers spend a lot of time and money on online magazines and sites that appeal to women. And because companies and ad agencies are run by men, they need to find out what women want and how to sell to women. And that's an opportunity for you.

So if the above is true, why aren't women creating, designing, and owning these areas?

You can try this at home for little or no money.

Learn programming.

Educate yourself. You have an advantage, if you can pinpoint it. You are the buyer. Sell to yourself.

This female-dominated marketplace should be teeming with female programmers.

And yet the vast majority of programmers are men.

Try this.

Your name is Victoria Fitzgerald. You're divorced, but your maiden (last) name is too Eastern European for most people to pronounce easily, so you decide to keep your ex-husband's name. Smart move. Less of a hurdle for someone to remember or try to pronounce your maiden name: Wyrzykowski.

Victoria Fitzgerald Apps. There. You just started a new company.

Employees? One. You.

Overhead? None.

Use your name in the title of your company. It's a free ride for YOU.

Get the dot-com domain.

Create a logo.

Trademark it, if you can.

Have a few hats and T-shirts made, and send them via FedEx to your Aunt Wyrzykowski in Vermont. Have Aunt Wyrzykowski send you five dollars for the T-shirt bearing your name and logo, so that it qualifies for the interstate commerce laws that will help you to shore up your trademark claim.

You should consult an attorney to make sure that all of your legal bases are covered.

And presto—you're in business.

You have nothing to lose. You have everything to gain.

Now, it's up to you to create, market, and sell to a marketplace dominated by your own kind: women.

Oh, you don't know much about programming?

Educate yourself online. Find out where they teach courses in programming. Or you can enroll in programming classes (try Dev Bootcamp, or Girls Who Code). And there are books that will teach you how to create apps, and even how to create an app business.

Shannon even got into the lady entrepreneur game herself. She took me to the E3 Expo in Los Angeles. There the biggest names in gaming held their annual get-together to show off their latest wares. She intended for me to immerse myself in gaming. But she wound up going over to the head of Gogii Games, made a contact, and created an electronic game for herself: Shannon Tweed's Attack of the Groupies. You can download it and play it. How to get rid of groupies in one thousand ways. Oh boy.

My point is, there are many ways to make something from nothing. Cottage industries, or garage industries, start with nothing. Apple, Hewlett-Packard, Facebook, and KISS all started in garages. And if you do it right, you will reap the benefits. That means money, and lots of it.

You can do it.

There is a door of opportunity right in front of you.

It's got your name on it.

Now, go out there and rule the world.

THE ART OF MORE: PRINCIPLE #10

SEE, UNDERSTAND, AND EARN POWER

Power comes in many forms—overt power is obvious in our day-to-day interactions with other people. Police have power over the roads and streets. Teachers have power over their classrooms. Bus drivers have power over their passengers. But larger degrees of power can be more complex—a mild-mannered general wields far more power than a drill sergeant barking orders, just as a songwriter has more financial power than the artist performing his work.

Recognizing true power is a skill in its own right, and it can be leveraged to your advantage—especially in forming alliances with other Me, Inc.'s who share similar goals to your own.

22

Kid Entrepreneurs

"I started the site when I was nineteen.
I didn't know much about business back then."
MARK ZUCKERBERG
founder, chairman, and CEO of Facebook

I f you have kids, get them started on being entrepreneurs.

The old cliché—the lemonade stand—is a good place to start.

Your kids have to figure out how much lemons cost. How much sugar costs. They have to put in their own sweat equity, that is, work. They have to figure out how much to charge for their product so they will have a profit in the end. Also, where do they sell the lemonade to get in front of as many people as possible, and at what time?

Turn your kids' hobbies into an entrepreneurial project.

I did.

I bought and sold comic books, and made a few thousand dollars. That amount helped to pay for my college education.

A hobby, like stamp collecting, can quickly turn into a business.

Buying and selling people's unwanted attic clutter can turn into a business.

Steven Spielberg, whom I've had the pleasure of visiting at his home to recommend a good school for my children, began pursuing his hobby as a very young man. He grew up in Arizona, a good ways from the movie industry.

In his early teenage years, Spielberg began making his own 8 mm films. He taught himself to operate the camera and create special effects, and learned all about lighting, editing, and directing. He filmed train wrecks at home, using his Lionel train set. He also charged his friends twenty-five cents to view his home-filmed masterpieces. So, in addition to being the filmmaker, he became the distributor and the exhibitor.

When he was thirteen, Spielberg made his own forty-minute war film, *Escape to Nowhere*, about a World War II battle in East Africa. At sixteen, he wrote and directed his own 140-minute sci-fi epic, *Firelight*, which later provided the inspiration for his *Close Encounters of the Third Kind*. Spielberg shot *Firelight* on a budget of five hundred dollars, and actually got it shown in a local theater. He even saw a profit from the film: one dollar.

The rest is history, and Steven Spielberg is now the most successful filmmaker of all time, with such historic blockbusters as *Jaws*, *E.T.*, *The Color Purple*, and *Schindler's List* to his credit.

He grew up an Orthodox Jew in Middle America. He encountered anti-Semitism, including being routinely beaten up for being Jewish.

There wasn't a school for film where Spielberg lived, so he taught himself.

If thirteen-year-old Steven Spielberg had walked up to you and told you he was going to become the most celebrated film director in history, you'd think that was a silly or perhaps impossible notion.

But that's exactly what he did.

And it all started when he was a kid.

And it all started with a dream. A big one.

But none of it would have happened if that little kid who was beaten up for being Jewish and stayed in Middle America listened to the bullies or lamented his misfortune, and didn't make it happen for himself.

No one was going to do it for him. HE had to make it happen. So do you.

You're never too young to *make things happen* for yourself.

Don't give your kids a weekly allowance. Don't give your kids spending money. Give them a sense of pride by letting them create and run their own little business, hopefully making a profit. Let them become kid entrepreneurs.

We can also learn a thing or two from our children—the older we get, the less adventurous we tend to be. We rely on patterns and defaults that have brought us success in the past, even if they are no longer doing so. If you watch a child in action, they are constantly moving from one activity to the next, trying new things and often throwing caution to the wind.

As we take on more business and financial responsibility, caution becomes a virtue, but it can also be a burden as we try to keep our respective ships afloat.

Let's design a ship that won't sink, you say.

It's tough to do.

"Captain, I found a small pencil-thin hole in the hull of the ship."

"Don't worry, sailor, it will only let in a glass of seawater every hundred yards or so."

Of course, that ship will have sunk by the time it's reached its port. It doesn't take a lot. One hole can sink an entire ship.

So to design a ship, and a business model, that's virtually unsinkable, it's best to have lots of little ships tied next to each other, all of them going in the same direction and all carrying full loads, but not dependent on or "exposed" with the other ships. That way, if one ship sinks, the rest probably won't.

Or each section of your ship can be sealed off. If seawater comes flooding in, you can lock the steel doors and the water won't spread to the rest of the ship. There are some problems inherent in this model, but you get the idea.

It's better to be an octopus than a fish. If an octopus loses a tentacle to a predator, the octopus will survive with seven tentacles left to fend for itself, and perhaps a few lessons learned that will enable it to avoid another such attack. If a fish loses a fin—or worse, its tail—it's unlikely to fare as well and its survival will be questionable.

So use the Octopus Business Model.

Create non-cross-collateralized sections and/or businesses—which means that the *cost* of running a section of your business, and the potential *profit* of that business, should be self-contained, and not "cross over" to the other businesses. For instance, KISS is a band. It tours, has licensing and merchandising, and makes money. It also has costs in running the business. Gene Simmons is a non-crossed business entity. Gene Simmons is a partner in ROCK AND BREWS restaurant chain. The profits/costs of running KISS, do not cross over to the profits/costs of running ROCK AND BREWS, even though both KISS and ROCK AND BREWS share Gene Simmons. And if that one business is unprofitable, or is too time consuming or too labor intensive, get rid of it. Close it down. It will probably not affect the other businesses you have.

To keep with the nautical theme: Be an octopus. Cast a wide net. Spread your risk.

THE ART OF MORE: PRINCIPLE #11

STAY ADVENTUROUS

When you begin to find success, it's important to continue to take smart risks. Sitting back in a comfort zone will put you on a quick path back to where you started—broke. Maintaining your edge is essential.

23

Failure: What Doesn't Kill You Makes You Stronger

> "I've missed more than nine thousand shots in my career. I've lost almost three hundred games. Twenty-six times I've been trusted to take the game-winning shot and missed. I've failed over and over and over again in my life. And that is why I succeed."
> **MICHAEL JORDAN**
> basketball superstar, entrepreneur, and majority owner of NBA team the Charlotte Hornets

I 've got some bad news for you: you *will* fail.

But every time you fail, you will learn something.

Don't feel bad when you fail. You're no different than the most powerful, the most intelligent, and the most entrepreneurial among us.

When you buy a car, it comes with five wheels. The spare isn't there for *if* you get a flat tire—it is there for *when* you get a flat tire. Because you will get one. The car company expects you'll get a flat tire at some point. But as long as you've got a spare tire in the trunk, you can keep going.

In other words, you need to have a backup plan. Always.

When Paul Stanley and I put Wicked Lester together, we actually succeeded in getting a contract with Epic Records. But we failed to pick the right members for the band, and we failed to pick the right kind of music to make. So at the very beginning, we knew that we had failed.

So we adjusted.

We quit the band.

We formed a new band.

We changed the style of music.

We changed the personnel and persona of the band.

We looked at the marketplace of 1972 and noticed that the English glitter and glam bands were making the most noise. So we decided to put together our own version of that. We loved it, anyway. We paid attention to the market, but we also did something we truly loved. There's a balance there.

And after that first failure, we succeeded.

That was forty years ago.

If we hadn't failed and caught the mistake early enough, Wicked Lester would have come and gone, and we may have never had another chance at success.

Oprah Winfrey was fired as a young reporter, and then fired again as a co-anchor of a news show. Oprah Winfrey failed.

Walt Disney, in his early years, was fired by the newspaper he worked for. And his first attempt at a cartoon studio went bankrupt. Walt Disney failed.

Henry Ford changed the automobile industry by inventing the modern assembly line, but his first car company went bankrupt. And when he formed another car company, he failed again, and was fired from his own company. Henry Ford failed.

Donald Trump's hotel/casino business went bankrupt. And then when he tried again, his company went bankrupt again. Donald Trump failed.

Bill Gates, one of the richest men in the world, initially started off in a tech venture that quickly went belly-up. Bill Gates failed.

So when you fail (and you will), you will be in good company. All of these men and women have gone on to do great things. Their achievements speak for themselves. But don't think for a second the richest and most powerful people in the world have never failed. They have failed more times than they have succeeded. Just like you and me.

Not only have I failed more times than I have succeeded—I fail every day.

Read that again: every day.

Any success you see from me is built upon the bedrock of the corpses of other ventures that simply didn't work out, for one reason or another.

Those old adages about falling off the horse and getting back on again—those old clichés, "if at first you don't succeed," and the like—consider them again, as if for the first time. There is a reason they became clichés—you simply cannot survive as a businesswoman or businessman without them. If failure discourages you from being productive, you shouldn't bother becoming an entrepreneur.

You *will* fail. And then you will fail again. Over, and over, and over.

Simmons Records first saw the light of day when I met RCA Records head Bob Buziak and RCA International head Heinz Henn in the late eighties. All of us thought that I could repeat the success of my gut instincts. That refers to my having discovered Van Halen in 1978, and ignoring everyone in the peanut gallery who didn't believe in them. I signed Van Halen to my production company, Man Of 1,000 Faces, Inc., and flew them to New York to record a fifteen-song demo on a twenty-four-track tape. I produced that demo at Jimi Hendrix's Electric Lady Studios and used engineer Dave Wittman, who had worked on Humble

Pie and KISS records. The demo consisted of most of the songs on the first Van Halen album, and some that appeared on their later albums.

Our manager at the time, Bill Aucoin, didn't believe in Van Halen, and neither did any of my band mates. I wanted us to take Van Halen under our wing, and have them as the opening act on every one of our concerts. That would have instantly launched them, and given KISS an ancillary income stream from another band. At least that was the idea. But ideas are fragile. And unless you have like-minded people around you who believe, ideas tend to die. And so it did.

I let Van Halen go. I tore up the contract that tied them to me. I felt that I had to do that on an ethical basis. Within six months, Van Halen would sign with Warner Bros. Records, and the rest is history.

My experience with Van Halen had a big influence in my launching of Simmons Records. Never again would a band slip through my fingers because others didn't believe. At least that was the idea when Buziak, Henn, and I agreed to start the label.

Initially, there was some traction. The label's first act was a new band led by Gregg Giuffria, who previously played keyboards in another band I discovered: Angel. When I first saw Angel at a club in Washington, D.C., I immediately called Casablanca Records president Neil Bogart, and in short order, Angel got signed to the label.

After Angel, Gregg had gone off on his own and started another band called Giuffria. They were on MCA Records. Their contract was up, and Gregg wanted to move his group to another label. I was interested, but I thought that the name of his band didn't resonate. That's putting it mildly. I insisted it had to be changed; otherwise I wouldn't sign the band. I created and trademarked the name "House of Lords" and gave it to the band to use. No fee. No percentages taken. House of Lords signed with Simmons/RCA Records and two albums were released. Medium success. Not what I wanted. I wanted BIG.

I then signed a Southern California band called Silent Rage. I called Black Sabbath's manager at the time, and got Rage an opening slot on their tour.

And finally, Buziak asked me to sign a band he believed in from Canada called Gypsy Rose.

Eventually, Simmons Records and RCA parted company.

By the nineties, KISS had reunited with Peter Criss and Ace Frehley and toured the world to become the number-one tour. KISS was without a record company at the time. At the same time, I had cowritten songs with Bob Dylan and Frank Zappa and wanted to release those songs. They weren't right for a KISS album, but a solo album would solve that dilemma. I started talking with Sanctuary Music about a Gene Simmons solo album and the relaunch of Simmons Records and I made a two-pronged deal. One was to relaunch Simmons Records and debut it with a Simmons solo album. And the other was to find a home for new KISS albums. Once they agreed in principle, I handed over the KISS recording rights to our new manager, Doc McGhee. Eventually, that would result in our worldwide bestselling album and video, *KISS Symphony*.

But the debut Simmons/Sanctuary release was my solo album, which I titled *Asshole*. The title was a lapse of judgment. There was a song on the album called "Asshole," and at the time I thought that an in-your-face title would get people's attention. It didn't.

I also released an album by a multitalented Canadian artist named Bag. The album didn't do well.

But I play that album to this day.

Eventually, Simmons Records and Sanctuary Music parted company as well.

Then I met Randy Lennox of Universal Records Canada. We had a meeting of the minds, and we agreed to relaunch Simmons Records with a new mandate: find the next big bands from Canada. The first signing was a great little band from Toronto called the Envy. I loved 'em. Headed by lead singer Shaun Frank and guitarist Void, the band went on to open an entire North American/Mexican KISS tour. They opened for us on forty shows.

But the music industry had changed drastically. It had become very difficult to launch a new band. Music was routinely being downloaded and file-shared for free. Record companies were going out of business, one after the other. And despite the quality of the songs on the Envy's debut album and despite their live-performance prowess, the band failed to get traction.

I then met Brittany Paige. She wrote real metal songs and fronted a band called Kobra & the Lotus. I loved what I saw and heard. But I wouldn't budge on insisting she get rid of the name Brittany. The name would always bring to mind one of the biggest-selling female singers of the time—Britney Spears—and it clearly wasn't a metal name. I insisted she change her name to Kobra Paige. That one move would connect the singer with the name of the band. I arranged European and South American festival concert dates for the band to play in front of other big metal bands. And we are getting some traction. Kobra is currently recording its second album. We could fail. Who knows?

Although my contract stipulates I could have signed up to six additional bands, I decided to concentrate on less rather than more. There *are* new bands that have the goods. But it takes so much money and hard work to launch a single act that taking on too many new acts would undermine chances of success.

Simmons/Universal Records continues.

I was a fan of the comic book *Jon Sable*, by Mike Grell. The origin of the character had to do with a young boy who grew up in the wilds of Africa. His father, a big-game warden, and his family are killed by poachers and diamond hustlers. The little boy grows up without parents and moves to New York, where he hires his services as a big-game hunter in the concrete jungle.

I was able to get the rights to the comic book, and set it up with film company InterMedia. I got Steven de Souza (*Die Hard*) to write the script. We were going out to Pierce Brosnan to star, and then everything fell apart, as so often happened. That's why they call it development hell. Few projects ever make it to the screen.

In a strange twist of fate, *Jon Sable* resurfaced, this time as a TV series project. Director/writer Gary Sherman, who directed me in *Wanted Dead or Alive*, was to direct the *Jon Sable* TV series. And perhaps because we enjoyed working together on that movie, Sherman offered me the part of Sable. I flew out to Chicago and met my costar, a young model who was just getting started in her acting career: Rene Russo. We shot the pilot and . . . I was terrible. I simply didn't come off well. I was let go, and I went back on tour with the band.

Even with all the glitz and glam, even after KISS's rise to fame and fortune, I failed in the most rookie of ways. Over and over.

Incidentally, the *Jon Sable* TV series actually saw the light of day on ABC, but only lasted six episodes.

One day, when all the dust settles and I come up for air, I may revisit the Sable story.

Stay tuned.

Gene Simmons Tongue magazine started as an idea I first dreamed up as a teenager. I had published fanzines devoted to sci-fi, fantasy, movies, comics, and the like: *Cosmos*, *Faun*, *Tinderbox* and others. I self-published, wrote, edited, and distributed them. Good experience for what was to come later. Sterling/Macfadden publishing had often put out KISS-related magazines, and they always did well. Head publisher Allen Tuller and I became friends and started talking about doing a magazine together. *Gene Simmons Tongue* would be a natural extension of my interests in pop culture and a celebration of life.

As I mentioned earlier, we lasted five issues. The magazine world was in turmoil at the time, and publishing in general was going head-to-head with the Internet. Newspapers and magazines were going out of business, left and right.

But I'm proud to say that during our run, I interviewed Hugh Hefner, who graciously allowed us to premiere our magazine with him on the cover, as well as Sir Richard Branson, Marvel's Avi Arad, Roseanne, Snoop Dogg, and many others.

Will we do it again?

Stay tuned.

As *Gene Simmons Tongue* magazine was coming to an end, I started doing research and found that the electronic gaming world is many times bigger than the film world. So much so, that Black Ops and Soldier of Fortune and Grand Theft Auto outgross the biggest movies. And each one of these games sells for about fifty dollars new. So I looked into either starting another magazine, or morphing *Gene Simmons Tongue* into a new mag. The result was the planned *Gene Simmons Game* magazine. I also trademarked it. There was a business plan drawn up and some articles written, but honestly, I became so busy with other things, and the magazine world was, again, a difficult place to find success. I had to put it to the side for another day.

When I have some time, I intend on revisiting *Gene Simmons Game.*

Meanwhile, my Simmons Comics Group banner has given birth to three titles that I created and trademarked:

Gene Simmons House of Horrors™, which is currently being developed by Georgeville/Reliance for a TV anthology series, with yours truly hosting. Eli Roth has been given an offer to be the show runner.

Zipper™ is likewise being developed as a scripted TV show by Georgeville/Reliance. *Zipper* is the story of a stranger in a strange land, an alien with Shakespearean overtones.

Dominatrix™—surprisingly, no one had trademarked the title, so I did—has garnered the interest of filmmaker Marc Forster, who directed *World War Z*. We are currently developing it as a film.

I have high hopes for these ventures. By the time this book is published, perhaps I will have succeeded. Perhaps I will have failed, with one or all of them.

Welcome to life.

I'm also working on launching my own rock music festivals around the country. Everything takes time, and so will this.

Titans of Rock™ (notice the trademark) almost launched when I was asked to headline the Rock and Roll All Stars tour of South America. But the people behind it decided to keep the All Stars name. Generic, I thought. But, onward.

I designed and trademarked both the logo and the name. You will see it happen. Soon. With luck, and work.

The reason I'm telling you all this is that you must understand how relentless you have to be. To be an entrepreneur, and simply to be alive—since life *is* business. You will not only fail, you will fail miserably. And you will fail again. And again. And again. If the laundry list of ventures above felt exhausting to you, that's because your ventures will be exhausting. You will want to get discouraged. You will have a string of failures so consistent that it will seem like the world is working against you.

This is normal. Pay it no mind.

The next venture, and the next, and the next, you must attack with the very same ferocity, the very same enthusiasm, and the very same delusional faith in yourself as you had when you began your very first. Never slow down, even for a moment. It only takes one success to make all the failures worthwhile.

Like I said above—stay tuned. All of these might fail. Or some of them might succeed. Or all of them might succeed. No matter what happens—I will continue pushing relentlessly. And so must you.

THE ART OF MORE: PRINCIPLE #12

KNOW WHEN TO PULL THE PLUG

I fail all the time. It means nothing. But a crucial, learnable skill is having the ability to fail and pick yourself back up. It will make you more successful, and in order to be a smart and reputable business person you have to know when something isn't working, and when it's time to give it up.

Take a cue from the best athletes in the world. "What doesn't kill you makes you stronger" is actually a really good phrase. If you're alive, you're in the game. Every time you fail you learn something, and next time you won't make that mistake again.

24

Investing

"Every day I get up and look through the *Forbes* list of the
richest people in America. If I'm not there, I go to work."
ROBERT ORBEN
comedy writer, author, magician, and
speechwriter for President Gerald R. Ford

nvest in the stock market

Invest in your future.

Invest in yourself.

I always made sure I saved anywhere from 25 to 50 percent of every dollar I made. I still do.

Remember, we all have to pay taxes, so that whittles the amount we earn down by as much as half before you decide whether to spend or save your money.

Always live below your means.

I'm like you. I wasn't educated in these areas. And they never taught me any of this in public school.

When I was twelve, at my mother's urging I opened up my first savings account in a local bank. It was a good idea. Money I didn't have in my pocket would be money that I wouldn't spend, especially on things I really didn't need. Eventually, I noticed over time that I actually *made* a little bit of money in my account. It was called "interest."

As I accumulated more money, I also saved more. I started learning about things like inflation. And how prices of everything seem to keep going up and up. Inflation means the decrease in the actual value of money. Simply put, ten cents no longer gets you into a movie theater. Nor will a dollar. It's now increasingly common to pay ten dollars or more for a movie ticket.

When you combine the fact that a dollar loses value every year and things cost more every year, it becomes clear that savings accounts in banks will only do so much for you. They simply don't earn enough interest to make up for the rise of the cost of things and the rate of inflation.

I had to learn about the stock market.

When I first started reading about it in newspapers and books, it seemed no different than learning Mandarin Chinese.

It was difficult to learn, but I had to do it.

If you've built up a decent amount of cash that you don't need to pay your bills with, you might consider investing in the stock market. Millions do.

Early on, I learned about spreading the risk, mutual funds, and the Dow Jones Industrials, aka "the Dow." And penny stocks. And futures. And commodities.

You don't have to learn all of that, but it helps if you do.

So let's simplify.

You're twenty-five to thirty years old.

You've been able to save $40,000, after tax. I commend you. That means that you've already paid your tax. You've already paid your bills.

And remember, I'm a novice, just like you are. I am not a trained accountant or a financial or business adviser. These are just my opinions. I have to say that to minimize my legal risk. (I don't wanna get sued. Who does?)

You will need to keep some cash handy, in case there's an emergency (this is known as being somewhat "liquid"). After you pay your bills and your tax, keep 10 percent "play money." But don't keep too much cash around. You will spend it.

You may decide to invest the rest of your money. If so, get some professional advice. Some investments may punish you if you take out the cash too early. You may have to wait a certain period until the investment "matures" in order to withdraw the cash. Which is good, because we are told that the longer you stay in the market, the better your chances of making money by investing.

Take the remaining money and invest in the stock market. Get a financial adviser, and ask about mutual funds.

Mutual funds sprinkle your dollars across a few different investments. In the game of roulette, they tell you not to bet all of your chips on one number. It's also known as not putting all of your eggs in one basket. The simple idea is that if something goes wrong with one investment—and it certainly can—you still have other investments that will hopefully make up for the loss and keep you in the profit margin.

Spreading the risk means exactly that. Some of your investments will go up. Some will go down. Hopefully, the overall number will give you an increase—a profit—above the rate of inflation (that is, larger than the rate at which the dollar is losing value).

I've done well in the stock market. In fact, it has made me quite a bit of money.

In 2009, I was invited by the New York Stock Exchange to ring the bell at the start of the trading day. It was a proud moment. I never imagined that I would wind up there, let alone that I would be there by invitation. As it happens, the former head of the New York Stock Exchange was a classmate of mine in high school. And when I came down to the NYSE, the media was there. Photographers were there. And our TV show, *Gene Simmons Family Jewels*, filmed the event.

From my vantage point above the trading floor of the world's trading center, I was reminded that I came to America as a legal immigrant with my mother, and step by step, day after day, worked to get where I was. Tears almost rolled down my face, and I was grateful to America and its people for allowing me all of this. I was humbled.

I know—the big bad capitalist actually had an emotional connection to the money game. Strange, isn't it, since guys like me are always portrayed as the villain? That is because my preoccupation with money comes from somewhere real—it comes from buying my mother a house, making her comfortable. It comes from putting as large a wall as possible between myself, my children, and starvation. Doesn't sound quite like the evil CEOs you so often hear about, does it?

Around 2008, the marketplace was unhealthy. It was the beginning of a period of big plunges in the real estate market, with people and banks both getting hurt. The Dow (meaning the stock market) was right under 8,000 points then. That number was bad. It signaled a very bad time for the investment community, and a general lack of health in America's economy.

As I was leaving, I walked the floor of the New York Stock Exchange, and there were photographers and TV crews shooting there. One news outlet, Fox Business, asked me what my view was regarding our economy in general, and about the Dow being in the unhealthy neighborhood of 7,800.

My answer, in so many words, was this: I don't know about you, but I'm investing in America. I am taking all of the money that I stupidly waste throughout the year, and instead of throwing it away, I'm investing in the stock market. In biotech, in food, in McDonald's, in Coca-Cola. Take all your stupid money, and don't throw it away on needless things. Take it and invest in yourself—invest in America.

If you followed my point of view, and had a little gut instinct and luck, you would have *doubled* your investment in just a few years with picks of a few of the right stocks. Today, the Dow is over 17,000.

So, what level of money should you invest in the stock market? Use your own judgment. Seek sound advice.

Consider all the times you went to a bar or restaurant and treated your friends. Think about all the trips and vacations you've taken. Afterward, you may have wished that you hadn't taken that trip or vacation. I would suggest that if you'd taken all the money that you spent on clothes/shoes/electronics/cars/houses (with after-tax dollars, remember), and *invested* it instead of spending it, you'd be a lot better off.

Remember, once you've spent money, you will never see it again.

But, if you invest money, you will probably see a profit, and pay tax only on the capital gain, meaning, the profit that you made on the money that you would have spent otherwise. See?

You will also have to invest in your individual retirement account (IRA), but your employer can help there.

You will also need to have insurance. Health insurance. All sorts of insurance.

These are things you need.

The shoes/electronic gadgets/cars are things you don't need. Not when you're starting out.

Invest in America.

Invest in what you know.

Invest in yourself.

THE ART OF MORE: PRINCIPLE #13

KNOW WHEN TO DOUBLE DOWN

The key to ascending to the highest heights of success is to know when to increase your efforts toward an already successful enterprise. This is what separates the men from the boys, the truly rich from the successful, and leads toward achievements beyond even your original hopes and dreams.

25

In Summary

"You miss one hundred percent of the shots you don't take."
WAYNE GRETZKY
"the Great One," widely considered the greatest hockey player of all time

hope this book has been a good kick in the pants.

I wrote this book because public school never taught me what I needed to know to succeed in life. School did give me some basics. I can read. I can write. I know historical facts. But remembering antiquated dates never helped me pay my bills, nor fulfill my entrepreneurial dreams.

I had to teach myself what I needed to know. So will you.

I had to reinvent myself. So will you.

I had to figure out what worked. So will you.

I hope this book has given you the ABC's of how to become an entrepreneur.

I know you want to become one. A successful one. That's why you bought this book in the first place.

By the time you get to this point in the book, you will have noticed that most of it focuses on YOU. And I will have said many things that might upset you. And I apologize to any whose feelings I have hurt.

But it's called *business*, not friends.

Friends tell you what you want to hear. And are kind.

Business doesn't care what you want to hear and doesn't care if you think it's kind.

In fact, business can fire you.

And often it does.

You know what you shouldn't do in life, but you keep on doing it.

I know I shouldn't eat carbs, but I sometimes do. And when I get fatter, I need a trainer to get me to the gym to work it off.

You know you shouldn't smoke, use drugs or drink, or get married young, or do any of the other stupid things you do. But the majority of you keep doing it anyway.

But if the only thing this book does is change what you take for granted, make you reassess your life decisions, and remind you that it's all up to YOU to make yourself successful, then I did my job.

In the real world, once you grow up and Mom or Dad isn't there to bail you out of trouble, there is no one there to help. And there will be no one there to force YOU to lead a smart life. And an economical life. And have a lifelong business plan.

YOU will have to do that for yourself.

But here's the good news: YOU will get all the rewards.

And take heed, regardless of your age: it's never too late to get started.

It's never too late to get started NOW.

Despite the fact that I just wrote a book about it, there are no hard rules for the secrets of success.

If there were, everyone would be successful, and we would all follow those clear-cut steps. What this book provides are guidelines, what worked for me, and what has worked for others.

But there are no shortcuts. Forget the "10 Rules for Success."

You will *have* to educate yourself in areas public schools did not.

You will *have* to be your own taskmaster.

This book is the first step.

Keep it by your nightstand or by your toilet, wherever you do your reading.

Please come back to it to keep reminding yourself what you need to do.

This is certainly not all of it. There is more. And there will always be more.

And here's a happy thought: You don't have to be all that qualified to be a real entrepreneur. You can learn what you need to learn by doing. However, as in most things in life, *you'll* have to do it. No one else will do it for you.

Without core values, and self-determination and self-restraint (no drugs, booze, tobacco, and stay away from people who engage in that stuff), and just plain "street smarts," you will get nowhere. Fast.

I wish you health. I wish you happiness. And, I wish you success in your journey to fulfilling your entrepreneurial goals.

This is not the end.

This is the beginning of the rest of your life.

Now, go get 'em.

ACKNOWLEDGMENTS

To the KISS Army, who made it all possible. I hope you'll find tools in this book to improve your life.

To Paul Stanley, who stuck it out with me through thick and thin.

Thank you: Jud Laghi, Nick Simmons for your editorial help, and to you reading this book, for making my life possible.

GENE
SIMMONS

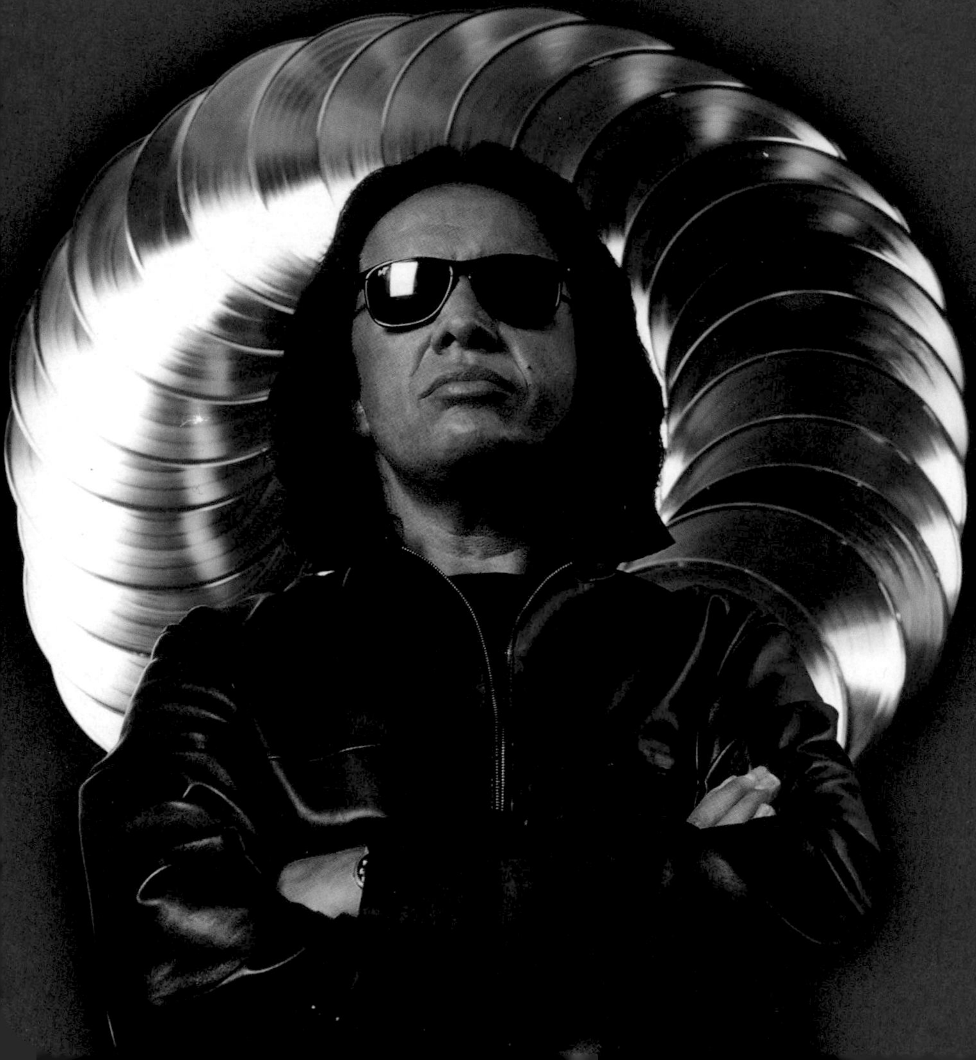